Decorating with Wild Flowers

· CYNTHIA VENN ·

· ACKNOWLEDGEMENTS ·

To my Husband Rob.
Thank you for your constant support and
for your valuable contribution to this book.

The Author would also like to thank the following for their assistance:

Pettinice used for covering the cakes:
British Bakels Ltd, 238 Bath Road, Slough SL1 4DU

Perspex Stand: Cake Art Ltd, Unit 16 Crown Court,
Crown Industrial Estate, Priors Wood, Taunton TR2 8RX.

'L' Brackets used in Floating Extension Work:
Linda Wong, 1 Purcell Avenue, Tonbridge, Kent.
For a comprehensive guide to extension work, see *Floating on Air* by Linda Wong.

Latex for Moulds: Midland Icing Centre, 0922 410040

Steel Cakestands: Cynthia Venn, 3 Anker Lane, Stubbington, Hants. PO14 3HF.

Decorating with Wild Flowers by Cynthia Venn

Illustrator: Robert J. Venn

Photographer: Trevor Juniper LBIPP LMPA, Portsmouth.

First published in 1992 by Cynthia Venn, 3 Anker Lane, Stubbington, Fareham, Hants. PO14 3HF, England.

Copyright © Cynthia Venn 1992.

ISBN 0 951 8913 0 8

Book Design & Production: Woodfield Publishing Services, Fontwell, West Sussex, England

Printed in Great Britain

· CONTENTS ·

·THE AUTHOR·

Cynthia Venn's interest in Sugarcraft began in 1975 following a three-day comprehensive course in Royal Icing techniques. The acquired skills were quickly put to good use in the production and sale of wedding cakes and in teaching the craft to students at local Further Education classes.

An introduction to the British Sugarcraft Guild whose aim is to share ideas and develop skills made her realise that practically anything can be crafted from sugar. A basic course in flower making with Tombi Peck taught her the techniques required for modelling flowers and it is this particular form of sugarcraft which has given her most pleasure and reward.

Cynthia has won several National competitions including Masterclass awards and is now a British Sugarcraft Guild judge. She travels widely around the British Isles teaching and demonstrating. She is a frequent visitor to the U.S.A. and has enjoyed visiting many States teaching, demonstrating and promoting her books.

Cynthia's first introduction to publishing was to contribute to the *International School of Sugarcraft Pt.II* (Merehurst). Her first solo book was *Christening Cakes* (Merehurst) followed by *Floral Designs for Cakes* (Merehurst) and lastly, due to her work in adapting smocking skills to sugarcraft *Smocking in Sugarpaste* (Merehurst). She also runs a business, designing and marketing specialised sugarcraft equipment.

Cynthia's love of the countryside and the beauty of natural flowers has inspired her to write *Decorating with Wild Flowers*. She spent many months researching the habits, botanical details and folklore associated with many common flowers. Her attention to detail and the subtleties of colour are all clearly defined and illustrated in this, her latest book.

Photograph by R.B. Freemantle

·INTRODUCTION·

I know a bank whereon the wild thyme blows
where oxlips and the nodding violet grow
Quite over-canopied with luscious woodbine;
with sweet musk roses and with eglantine.

William Shakespeare
A Midsummer Night's Dream

These magical words portray a beautiful country scene of bygone times when the meadows, woods and hedgerows were richly decorated with a vast array of wild flowers, fruits and herbs. Sadly, a scene such as this is no longer commonplace in the late 20th Century except to a few fortunate country-dwellers living in remote areas.

Widespread use of herbicides and ruthless town planning have destroyed many beautiful wild flowers and a few, such as the cornflower, cowslip, fritilliary and others have almost become extinct. Members of the public are protesting in large numbers and many are fighting to preserve our heritage by campaigning against the destruction of beauty spots, by planting trees, and sowing wild flower seeds in their gardens which encourage and provide a haven for birds, butterflies and small mammals.

Schools are teaching small children to value and love wild flowers and more people are becoming educated enough to look, admire and possibly photograph but not to pick the rare wild flowers. Railway banks and the verges of motorways are host to a rich assortment of flowers and wildlife because of their inaccessibility to ramblers and crop sprayers.

There is a growing interest in all things pure and natural, from wholefoods to perfumes and health remedies. Herbal medicine is enjoying a revival of interest. It is no longer dismissed as 'quackery' and can be very safe, effective and free of side-effects when used for acute conditions. Toiletries and cosmetics made with natural perfumes are very popular, they do not irritate the skin and are mostly well tolerated by sensitive people.

Natural themes of simple flowers, berries and leaves are favourite choices for household fabrics, china and wallcoverings. Brides often choose wild flowers and simple country themes for their weddings. The theme can be continued by decorating the cake in an unsophisticated style and using sugar wild flowers. Many of the flowers featured in this book are common, a few are more rare.

Seasons are unpredictable and consequently wild flowers no longer seem to fit neatly into their traditional seasons. Warm Winters and cool Summers can result in Spring flowers appearing in Winter and Summer flowers still in evidence in late Autumn. This will allow more flexibility of choice when planning seasonal cakes.

Hollowing

Many of the flowers in this book are made without the use of cutters. Undoubtedly cutters are very useful tools – particularly when a lot of flowers are required and time is short – but with a little practice it is possible to make many small flowers more realistic by the hollowing method and it is a technique well worth mastering.

Tools required for the hollowing method are:
- Small pointed scissors
- Cocktail sticks (thin modelling sticks)
- Modelling tools – small & medium ball tools or dog bone tool, pointed tool
- Small knitting needle (cable needle)
- Paintbrush, wires, fine stamens.

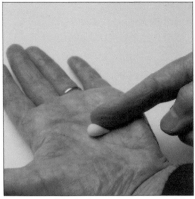

1. Roll small ball of paste into a cone. If the paste has a tendency to stick to the hands or the modelling stick, use a little cornflour (cornstarch).

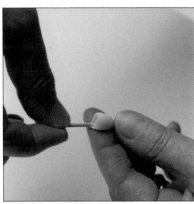

2. Hollow by inserting cocktail stick. Rotate cone against the side of the index finger with the stick inside until the walls are very thin.

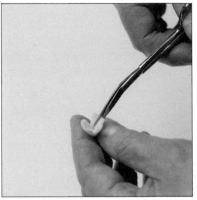

3. Cut the required number of petals with small pointed scissors.

4. Open out and trim off square corners.

5. Thin and improve petal shape by laying over a finger and rolling with a modelling stick – especially the edges.

6. Insert hooked wire and stamens. Finish each flower according to individual instructions.

'Mexican Hat'

This term is widely used throughout the book and refers to a basic shape from which many flowers and sepals are cut. Form a ball of gum paste into a cone, this will vary according to the size required for the finished flower.

STEPS

1. Flatten the wider end of the cone between thumbs and fingers to form a flat disc.

2. Roll out from the centre with a paintbrush handle or small knitting needle until thin.

3. Using a hollow centred cutter, cut out the shape of the flower.

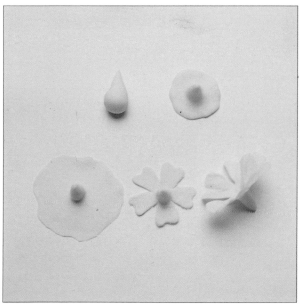

The 'Mexican hat' method.

Making Stamens

It is not always possible to purchase very fine stamens and where masses of stamens are required for a certain flower, or a particularly unusual shade is required, home-made stamens are very effective.

● Using sewing thread, wind around two fingers several times. This will vary according to the number of stamens required for a particular flower.

● Remove the circle of cotton from the fingers and twist a length of fine wire through the loops as in diagram below.

● Cut through the threads, leaving the length of cottons you need for the stamens.

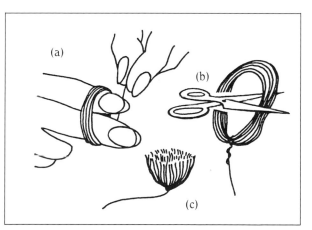

(a) Winding cotton around fingers. (b) Cutting cottons the length required. (c) Wired stamens ready for use.

Making Leaves

Colouring

Make your leaves from a lighter green than you want the finished leaf to be, this will allow you complete freedom to brush on deeper shading where it is required to give a lifelike appearance to the leaf. Dust the centre slightly darker than the outside edge to emphasise that the central vein is recessed.

Some leaves (e.g. the Rose) have russet shading. This can be achieved by lightly brushing with red colour, the green of the leaf underneath the red will bring out the russet tones.

Make Autumn leaves pale gold, this is a very good base colour to take the shades of red, green, or brown which can be brushed onto the finished leaf.

Some leaves (e.g. Ivy) are dark green with lighter veins. Make the leaf the paler colour you want the veins to be and paint or dust the darker green onto the areas in between, showing up the paler veins.

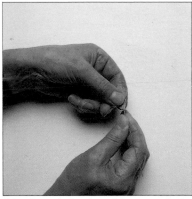

1. Roll the paste thin leaving a thickened ridge in the centre.

2. Cut out shape, arranging the cutter or template so that the thickened ridge is at the base of the leaf.

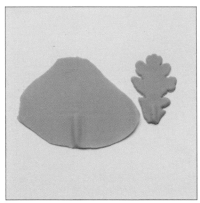

3. Vein leaf with appropriate veiner.
Using a small ball tool, thin the edge of the leaf.

4. Dip the end of a piece of fine covered wire into egg white or gum glue and carefully push it into the thickened area of the leaf. Press firmly to secure.

5. Pinch the back of the leaf along the central vein to emphasise it. Turn back the edges into a natural curve. Dry supported in a realistically curved shape.

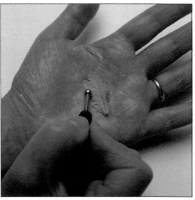

6. Dust with edible powder colours to shade, then glaze.

Leaves consisting of several sections and complicated shapes such as the Buttercup, Meadow Cranesbill and Wood Anemone, are best made in two or more sections using 30 or 33g wire and taped together when dry.

Where you have access to a real leaf and can make a mould for veining, it will not be necessary to use a cutter, provided the leaf is of a suitable size. Roll out the paste with a thickened ridge as usual. Press the veiner firmly on to the paste. Cut round the outline of the leaf with small pointed scissors. Turn the leaf over and, working from the back, thin the edge by stroking firmly with a small ball tool, taking care not to flatten the veins. To finish, refer to general instructions.

Glazing

This is the final step after the shading has been added. Most leaves need to be glazed, some have a very subtle sheen, others have a very glossy appearance. Take care not to add too much gloss, this gives an artificial look.

For a natural-looking, fairly matt effect, pass the surface of the leaf quickly over a steaming kettle. This will give a slight shine and allow the colours to blend well. Do not be deceived by the initial shiny appearance, this will be much less when the leaf is dry. DO NOT ALLOW CHILDREN TO USE THIS METHOD.

Gum Arabic glaze (see page 10) may be brushed over the surface of the leaf after colouring. Two coats may be necessary for very glossy leaves. The leaves might need re-glazing after a few months especially if they are not kept in a dry place.

A trace of vegetable fat rubbed over the leaf will also give a sheen.

Homemade Moulds for Veining

There are several ways of making simple veiners where the fibre of the original leaf is strong and has prominent veins. However, many leaves and petals are more delicately veined and the following method is particularly successful in these cases. You will need to make your collection of moulds when the particular leaf or flower is in bloom.

Latex Mould

Good moulds can be made quickly and easily by brushing the surface of a clean leaf with liquid latex. The advantage of these moulds is that they are light to carry around and do not take up a lot of space in a workbox.

● Stick the leaf onto a board with double-sided sticky tape, surface of the leaf uppermost, making sure it is completely flat.

● Brush evenly with liquid latex and allow to dry.

● Make about seven or eight applications, drying in between each one, until you feel the mould is thick enough.

When a leaf or petal has very fine veining, it is better to use the underside of the leaf where the veins are more prominent. Press the underside of the leaf into a piece of plasticine or modelling clay. Carefully remove the leaf and you should have a good impression of the negative veins. Brush a coat of latex directly onto the plasticine and continue building up layers as before. When the layers are thick enough, peel off and the veiner is ready for use.

If you prefer a thicker mould, press the leaf into the plasticine as before. Remove the leaf, leaving a good impression of the veins in the clay. Pinch the clay all round the leaf to form a wall without any gaps. Brush a layer of latex over the leaf impression, taking care to remove all bubbles. Allow to dry. The latex becomes clear when it is dry. Pour more latex into the mould to the required thickness. Allow to dry overnight or until the latex has lost its milky look.

Trim round the leaf shape with scissors. Rub both sides thoroughly in cornflour to prevent veiners sticking to each other.

Making a mould (veiner).

Recipes

The following are recipes for a number of important components referred to throughout this book.

Royal Icing

200g (7oz) icing (confectioner's) sugar

1 egg white (size 3) at room temperature

- Sieve icing sugar several times through a very fine sieve or a nylon stocking as even coarse grains of sugar will block fine tubes (tips).

- Stir the egg white in a grease-free basin to break it up. Add the sifted sugar to the egg white 5ml (a teaspoon) at a time, stirring well between each addition. Continue adding sugar and beating well by hand until the icing will hold its shape firmly when pulled into a peak. If you prefer to use dried albumen instead of egg whites, follow manufacturer's instructions.

- Many cake decorators consider that the addition of gum arabic and liquid glucose to the mixed icing will strengthen and add elasticity for extension work. It is advisable to try piping with and without the additional ingredients to decide which you prefer. The proportions for a 7oz quantity of icing would be 2.5ml (half teaspoon liquid glucose) and 1.25ml (quarter teaspoon) gum arabic. Stir well and allow to stand at least an hour before using.

Flower Modelling Paste

Although it is now possible to buy very good ready-made flower modelling paste, it is not available everywhere. I have always found that the following paste dries very hard and has excellent handling qualities.

450g (1lb/3 cups) icing (confectioners) sugar

10ml (2tsp) cornflour (cornstarch)

15ml (1tbsp) gum tragacanth

10ml (2tsp) powdered gelatine

25ml (5tsp) cold water

10ml (2tsp) white vegetable fat

10ml (2tsp) liquid glucose

1 egg white, size 2 (large)

- Sift the sugar, cornflour (cornstarch) and gum tragacanth into an ovenproof bowl. Heat gently in the oven or over a pan of boiling water until the sugar feels warm.

- Sprinkle the gelatine on to the water and leave to stand until the gelatine has absorbed all the water. Dissolve over hot water or in a microwave (Do not allow the mixture to boil as this would destroy the elasticity). Remove from the heat and add the fat and liquid glucose.

- Pour the liquids and the egg white into a well in the centre of the sugar. Mix in a heavy-duty electric mixer set at the lowest speed until the sugar has been incorporated. Increase the speed to maximum and mix until the paste is white and stringy. This will take about 5-10 minutes.

- Put the paste into a strong polythene bag and keep this in a lidded container in the refrigerator overnight. Cut off small pieces as you need them and keep the rest in the refrigerator.

Gum Arabic Glaze

15ml (3tsp) cold water

5ml (1 teasp) gum arabic

- Pour the water into a small heatproof pot. Sprinkle gum arabic onto the water. Place the pot in a saucepan of simmering water. Stir the mixture until it has dissolved.

- Store in a screw top jar and use to brush onto leaves to obtain a gloss.

- N.B. This is also a good 'glue' for attaching flower petals as an alternative to egg white.

Gum Paste Glue

This is a strong, sticky substance made from mashing together a little gum paste and egg white. Mix until it is soft and stringy. It is very useful for sticking petals which need a bit of extra help to 'hang on' and as it can be made from exactly the same colour paste as the flower, it is invaluable for invisible repairs to broken flowers when the petals are already dry.

Brush Embroidery

This technique can be effectively used with moulded flowers to create a three-dimensional effect, also to continue a particular flower theme on another area of a cake.

Royal Icing is used with a little piping gel added in proportions of one-quarter teaspoon gel to about 8oz royal icing. This will delay the drying process and give a longer working time.

Always start with the background and gradually work towards the front. The areas at the back should not be as bold as the foreground so use a light film of icing, building up pressure on the icing bag when working towards the front to make the foreground more prominent.

METHOD

- Transfer the outline of the design by embossing or by pricking through the pattern with a pin.

- Start work on areas in the distance. Pipe the outline with a No.1 or '0' icing tube (tip). Pipe an inner line.

- Brush with a damp paintbrush through the outer line to the centre in long sweeping strokes. The icing should be thicker at the edge, thinning out until it is just a wash in the centre.

- Work forward, using the same method, each new outline covering the rough edges of the petal or leaf behind it.

- Flowers at the front may be emphasised by piping a thicker inner line of icing to be brushed through.

- Prominent areas, such as the furled edges of petals are piped last of all, the outline is then filled with soft icing and it is not brushed through.

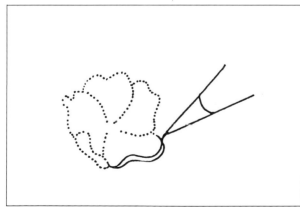

Piping outline of petal.

(a) Brushing through inner line.
(b) Emphasising furled edge of petal with extra icing.

Low Relief Arrangements

A low-relief arrangement is suitable for a framed picture or for the top of a cake.

A picture or flower arrangement can be made more interesting if the background is gradually faded out into the distance, the middle ground emphasised slightly, and the foreground made quite prominent. Many designs can be brought to life by adding a variety of textures in this manner. The flower picture illustrates this technique.

METHOD

- Draw or copy the design you intend to use. Study it well and mark the areas which will form the background, then mark the middle ground and the foreground.

- Transfer the design to the cake or plaque.

- Use a palette or white glazed tile to mix the paste or liquid food colourings, try to avoid using colour straight from the pot.

- Use a spare plaque to test shade and strength of each colour before applying them to your picture.

- A fairly dry brush should be used to avoid the surface texture of the cake becoming marked with too much water but bear in mind that sugar will quickly absorb any water on the brush. Practice will show you just how much water you should use.

- Paint the background using pale colours, this will allow you the freedom to highlight or shade some areas when the base colour is dry.

- Emphasise the mid-ground with brush embroidery, using a '0' icing tube (tip) where flowers and leaves are small.

- Petals look more delicate when piped with white icing. When brushing through, a touch of colour can be applied to the brush giving natural looking colouring to the petals. Green leaves should be piped in pale green and brushed through with a darker green applied to the brush. Be prepared to highlight and shade the work when it is dry.

- The foreground needs even more emphasis with moulded flowers or leaves and the size of these should be carefully chosen to fit into the scale of the picture.

- Some flowers, such as wild roses, can be made by making and drying the individual petals and assembling the flowers with a little icing on the cake. Other smaller flowers may be made as directed but omitting the wire.

- To assemble the moulded flowers and leaves, stick a tiny piece of modelling paste onto the cake in a suitable colour to blend into the background. Stick a few unwired leaves which will be under the flowers, into position lightly so that you can rearrange them until you are happy with the result. Add the main flowers.

- Do not stick too rigidly to your design. Be flexible enough to add a little extra if necessary.

- Even small flowers such as primroses will be about lcm higher than the surface of the cake leaving a gap behind. It may improve the resulting picture if a few sprigs of smaller flowers are added to bridge that gap.

1. The design to be transferred to cake top or plaque.

3. Middle ground emphasised by raising slightly with brush embroidery which is merely painting in icing.

2. The background has been painted lightly with a fine brush and dilute colours.

4. Moulded flowers and leaves complete the picture.

Arranging Flowers Naturally

Flowers usually do not grow completely straight. For each flower to thrive, it needs plenty of light, therefore, if it is crowded by foliage or other blooms it will bend its stem away from the others, sometimes to the extent that the stem can be parallel with the ground, but since the centre of the flower needs to attract the insects which pollinate it and needs light, it will always turn its head towards the light thus producing a curved stem.

- When your flowers are dry, bend the stems over the pad of your thumb to give a gentle curve.

- Study your subject by taking country walks or by reading the individual habits from good botany books. Note the leaf formation in relation to the flowers.

- Wild flowers look their best in an uncontrived, natural arrangement and although the base must be modified when necessary to fit into the theme of a cake, individual arrangements look attractive when they appear to be growing naturally. This means colouring and decorating the base with the colours of nature which are mainly a mixture of browns, greens, black and white. Dried leaves and little twigs and stones also help to provide a natural setting.

Three different methods of assembling flowers are as follows:

1. Cut a piece of card into the required shape. Make a cushion of modelling paste the same shade as the cake and stick onto the cardboard base. This will enable the flowers to be removed from the cake easily. Stick the wired flowers into the paste, curving the stems in a natural way. Arrange plenty of leaves around the base to balance and to cover the foundation.

2. Flowers with long stems and heavy heads can be difficult to arrange because they tend to fall over before the base is set. Props will help but these make the job of adjusting the position of the flowers difficult since the overall effect of the arrangement cannot be assessed until they are removed.

   The best way of coping with this situation is to use long stems and to bend the end of the stem into a circle or to attach another short piece of wire to the base to form a tripod. Either of these methods will form a little platform which can then be set into soft modelling paste. Several flowers can be arranged, with a layer of paste between them and they will not keel over. This method is very useful for arranging flowers such as bluebells and lily of the valley, where all the flowers grow on the same side of the stem and the weight tends to pull the stem over to one side.

3. At times it may be desirable to form the wild flowers into some type of spray. On these occasions try to avoid imprisoning them into stiff little bouquets festooned with bulky ribbon loops or net. This is not a good way to show simple flowers at their best.

   Instead of ribbons, make wired leaves. Leave all stems quite long and leave plenty of space between flowers and leaves. A simple bow of ribbon could be tied around the stems which will have been previously taped or wired together.

   A spray can also be set into a simple holder. Allow some of the small flowers to tumble casually towards the cake, interspersed with small leaves. Arrange leaves to cover the point where the holder is inserted into the cake.

· ARRANGING FLOWERS ·

Colour Effects

Colour is in itself a vast subject, and for those students who want to study the subject there are many books which give detailed and accurate information. Whereas all knowledge is valuable, it is not necessary to read the subject in great depth to achieve good results.

Experimenting with colour can be very rewarding and no amount of theory can help as much as the observation and study of nature's colour changes from one season to the next and from sunlight to shade.

Colours should not be used 'straight from the pot'. This produces a harsh, artificial result, not at all compatible with the natural world. Nature's colours are subtle, rich, delicate, but never harsh and it is possible to produce very realistic results with a little blending.

- The three *Primary colours* – red, blue and yellow, cannot be produced by mixing together other colours.

- *Secondary colours* are produced by mixing equal quantities of two primary colours, e.g.

  Violet = Red + Blue

  Green = Blue + Yellow

  Orange = Red + Yellow

- Other combinations of colours are called *Tertiary colours* and most colours used by the artist would be tertiary since colours seen in nature are a combination of many colours. For example, brown comes from mixing primary red with secondary green which in itself is made up of blue and yellow. A blue-green is made by mixing blue with green.

- Before using a colour, assess the quality and if it is not quite suitable, add a little of another colour to improve it. A common offender is green. If the green in the pot is too yellowy, remember the two primary colours to make green are blue and yellow, therefore just a speck of blue may be enough to give the green you need.

- To make a colour lighter, white is added and the result is a tint of that colour. For example, adding red to white icing will produce pink which is a tint of red. To take it a stage further you may want to produce mauve by adding blue, since red and blue make purple, and mauve is a tint of purple.

- To give a colour a darker tone, black is added, this produces a shade of that colour. When it is added to a strong colour, it will neutralise the intensity resulting in a more subdued version of that colour.

- When colouring moulded sugar flowers, try to study growing flowers and note that the colour varies in intensity from one part of the flower to another. This effect can be achieved by making the flower very pale or white and then dusting the dried flower with a stronger version of the colour. Note that buds and half-open flowers are usually a stronger colour than fully open flowers. Flowers are never a flat colour and will vary according to the direction and amount of light.

- Leaves are often lighter at the edges, some are mainly dark but have lighter veins. Some rose leaves have russet shading at the edges, this effect can be produced by brushing them with red dusting powder before glazing. Autumn tints vary from yellow through orange, red, brown. Make the leaf pale so that these colour changes can easily be produced by dusting or painting.

- Have fun with colours and if you produce a particularly pleasing shade make a note of the details for the next time. Eventually you will become used to the colour combinations and confident of successful results every time.

Acorns

There are many different varieties of Oak and they all bear acorns in the Autumn. The acorns are all similar but vary slightly in size and shape from one Oak to another. They grow mostly in pairs and whereas the acorns of the English Oak grow on long stalks, many others have short stalks or none at all. Colour varies from green, through gold to brown according to maturity.

They make a very attractive decoration for Autumn celebration cakes, teamed with berries or Autumn flowers.

Acorns.

METHOD

- Take a small ball of green or light brown paste and roll it into an egg-shape. Insert a hooked piece of 26g wire into the base.

- Take another ball of paste, slightly smaller. Push a medium ball tool into it to hollow into a shallow cup shape.

- Press the edges of the cup between finger and thumb to thin.

- Brush the centre with egg white or gum glue.

- Push wire through the cup and pull the nut firmly into place.

- Mould the cup neatly around the nut.

- To texture the cup, take a pair of pointed metal tweezers and make little pinches close together around the base, repeat in uneven rows until the cup is textured all over.

- Paint feint lines in a deeper colour down the length of the nut.

- When dry, brush the nut only with gum arabic glaze.

- Arrange acorns back to back, in pairs, surrounded by Oak leaves.

- Construct leaves according to the instructions on pages 8–9. Use the template below.

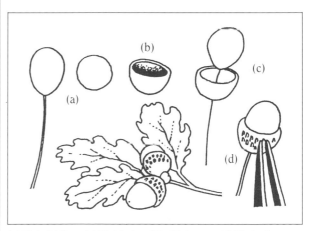

(a) Nut. (b) Cup. (c) Nut being fitted into cup. (d) Texturing cup.

Autumn Rabbit Cake

A seasonal cake featuring acorns, autumn leaves and a painted picture of rabbits.

METHOD

- Cut an oval plaque from modelling paste, measuring 7″ × 5″ (18cm × 12.5cm). Allow to dry and harden. Transfer the rabbit picture and paint (this is also suitable for cocoa painting).

- Brush an oval cake 10″ × 8″ (2.5cm × 20cm) with boiled, sieved apricot jam and cover with marzipan.

- Cover the top of the cake only with a disc of sugarpaste.

- Brush the sides and edges of the cake with alcohol such as gin or vodka, leaving the central area dry.

- Cover the whole cake with sugarpaste, smoothing it well to obtain a good surface. The template used for cutting the plaque can now be used to cut out an oval from the sugarpaste on top of the cake. Lift out the oval section and smooth the edges of the hollow top.

- Pipe beading around the base of the cake with a No. 2 icing tube (tip).

- Set the plaque into the hollow in the cake. Pipe a neat edge around the picture.

- Make several clusters of acorns and leaves.

- Make an assortment of leaves in rich Autumn colours. Glaze the leaves.

- Arrange small leaves and acorns around the edge of the picture, building up to a mass of leaves beneath the rabbits, cascading down the side of the cake. Add sprigs of acorns at board level.

Template for Autumn Rabbits.

· CYNTHIA VENN ·

Bindweed

This creeping or climbing plant is very troublesome to farmers because of its habit of wrapping itself around other plants and strangling them. It has pink and/or white flowers, five-petalled, but joined in a funnel shape.

The 'Hedge Bindweed' flowers April/July and climbs. The 'Field Bindweed' is smaller, creeps along the ground and has smaller flowers.

A very useful cake-decorating flower, it trails very prettily, mixes well with other flowers and its delicate colouring makes it a good choice for wedding cakes.

METHOD

- Take a pea-sized ball of white paste. Roll it into a cone shape. Insert a cocktail stick (modelling stick) into the wide end and hollow (*see page* 6). The cylinder will widen into a funnel shape and the walls will become very thin and transparent.

- Mark the funnel into five equal sections with a veining tool or blunt edge of a knife. Pinch at the back of each mark to reinforce the line. Coax the edges of the petals to turn back when making a fully open flower. For a half open flower, do not widen it so much.

- Push a hooked 30g wire through the throat of the flower and out through the base. Neaten the back. Push five short fine white stamens into the centre, grouping them close together.

- The calyx may be painted with mid-green food colouring as it is very small.

- Buds should be kept small, use about one-third of the amount of paste used to make the flower. Roll into a pointed cigar shape. Make several shallow cuts lengthwise down the bud. Push a hooked wire through the base. Paint calyx.

- When dry, brush the backs of the flowers pink or brush pale pink lines down each of the section lines. Touch the centre with a hint of yellow.

- Bind buds, leaves and flowers into a long trail, alternating each side of the stem.

Leaves

Cut the leaves out using a template or cutter and construct as shown on pages 8–9.

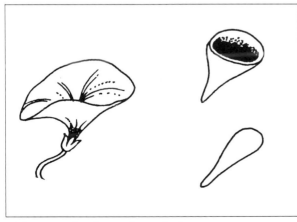

Hollowing and widening the petal tube.

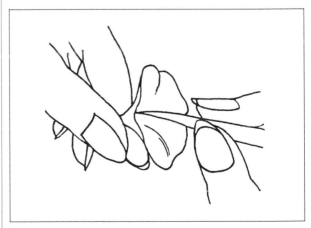

Veining.

· BINDWEED ·

Bluebell

The bluebell flowers April–June and carpets the woods and hedgerows with a lovely rich shade of blue, occasionally white. It is becoming less common and it is now illegal to dig it up. The biggest threat is from careless walkers trampling on the leaves more than from the pickers. The plant can survive without flowers but it will die from lack of food if its leaves are crushed.

The bulbs contain starch and this was used to stiffen the ruffs which privileged Elizabethans wore around their necks. The fragrant flowers are elongated and bell-shaped. They grow in a long one-sided spike, tapering to a cluster of buds and drooping at the tip. The fine bracts which grow from the base of the flower are coloured as for the flower.

The leaves are long, shiny and lance-shaped with a deep central groove. Both leaves and flowers grow straight from the root.

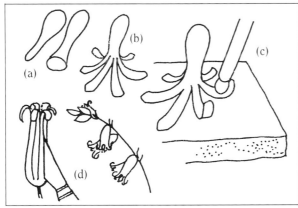

(a) Hollowed cone. (b) Petals cut. (c) Curling petals.
(d) Cutting division down to the bottom of the petal tube.

METHOD

Use blue paste to which has been added just a tinge of red. This will result in the mauvey-blue so typical of bluebells. If you keep the colour fairly pale you will be able to add interesting shading to the finished flower by brushing with a deeper blue-purple dusting powder, this will give a very lifelike appearance.

- Take a small ball of blue paste about $1/4''$ (6mm). Roll into a cone shape about $3/4''$ (2cm) long, tapering to a point at one end and leaving the base rounded.

- Insert a cocktail stick into the narrow end, about $3/4$ of the way down the tube. Hollow and thin the paste, leaving a thick area at the base (see 'Hollowing', Page 6).

- Make six deep cuts down the length of the tube, almost to the bottom of the cylinder. Snip off the square corners with a pair of small scissors.

- Lay the flower on its side and press each petal with a cocktail (modelling) stick to thin the edges.

- Curl back the tips of the petals by placing the flower upside down on a small piece of foam.

- Firmly press each tip with a small ball tool and stroke away from the tip; this will cause it to curl up.

- Push a piece of hooked 30g wire through the throat of the flower and out through the base.

- Cut ridges in the base of the flower extending the line of the petals.

- Shape the flower by drawing the petals up and pinching together to form a 'waist' just below the curled back tips.

- Brush a little egg white on the petals to hold them in this position but avoid the curled back tips.

- Add six fine stamens. (These are usually blue when the flower opens, turning yellow when the pollen appears.)

- Make several small pointed buds with half sized balls of blue paste. Mark ridges down the length of the bud.

- Tape buds and flowers together starting with buds and grouping the flowers on one side of stem.

- Cut fine blue bracts, add to the base of each flower stem.

·BLUEBELL·

Bramble

The Bramble flowers from May onwards and produces fruit until late Autumn. The delicate flowers with the dark, richly coloured berries make an excellent contrast and are popular with cake decorators.

METHOD

- **To make the blackberry**, colour a small amount of paste in various shades of red. A very strong red is required. Add a touch of black to darken. If the red is harsh, a little green will soften it.
- Take a small ball of dark red paste, about half the size required for the finished berry. Push a hooked 26g covered wire into the base.
- Roll some tiny balls of paste about 2-3mm in a mixture of medium and dark red. Stick to the main ball with egg white or gum, starting at the base around the wire.
- Repeat with the next row, staggering the berries so they are positioned in between the first row.
- Work until the ball is completely covered. These will stick more easily if they are attached to the central ball while they are still soft. Do not crowd them too much as this will cause them to dislodge each other.
- **To make the calyx**, roll out a small piece of light brownish-green paste very thinly.

- Cut out with a small star calyx. Thin the points with a ball tool.
- Attach to the base of the berry with egg white, press firmly against the base of the berry to encourage the points to fall back.
- **To make the flowers**, make stamens first, by cutting many short lengths of stamen cottons and binding them to a fine wire with tape. Brush this with green dust.
- Make a green calyx by making a Mexican Hat (page 7) and cutting with a small star or calyx cutter. Thin sepals with a small ball tool and insert a hooked 28 or 30g wire.
- Cut five small single petals with a miniature rose petal cutter. Thin the edges and cup with a small ball tool. Texture by pressing against fine petal veiner or a piece of corn husk.
- Lay each petal on the calyx with points to the centre. Push wired stamens through the centre. Surround the green cottons with a lot of very fine, brown-tipped stamens; these can easily be pushed into the paste while it is soft.
- **To make the leaves**, if possible vein with a natural veiner made from a real bramble leaf (see pages 8-9).
- Roll the paste out thinly and press against the mould. The impression of the shape of the leaf should be quite clear and can then be cut out with a small pair of pointed scissors.
- Tool the edge until very thin. Attach unhooked wire in the usual way. Alternatively leaves can be cut with rose leaf or Bramble cutters.
- **To assemble**, tape buds, flowers, berries and leaves together in a natural formation, refer to picture or a growing stem. Pipe thorns with greenish-brown Royal Icing and a '0' icing tube (tip).

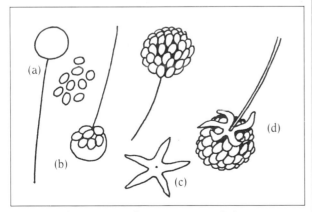

(a) Centre. (b) Berries stuck on to centre. (c) Calyx.
(d) Berry with calyx.

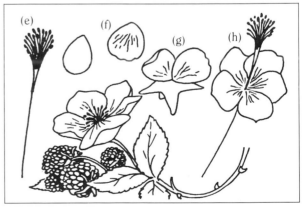

(e) Wired stamens. (f) Petals. (g) Petals arranged on calyx.
(h) Stamens pulled through flower centre.

·THE BRAMBLE·

Buttercup

A golden yellow flower with five shiny petals and a mass of stamens surrounding a pale green stigma. It is very common in meadows April-October but has only been known as buttercup since the 18th century. Before that it was the butterflower. It was once thought that the ground roots were a cure for the plague and that buttercups tied round the neck would also cure lunacy.

METHOD

The Stigma

- Take a tiny piece of pale green paste, make a cone shape and insert a 30g wire moistened with egg white. Allow to dry.

- Make stamens by cutting a thin strip of paste about $3/4''$ (2cm) long and $1/4''$ (6mm) wide. Cut one long

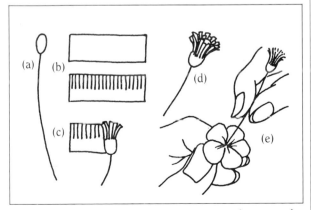

(a) Centre. (b) Stamens. Roll out narrow strip and cut one edge into a fringe. (c) Wind around centre. (d) Stamens, some curled in towards centre. (e) Stamens being inserted into flower.

edge into a very fine fringe (like a comb). Moisten the unfringed edge and wrap the strip around the centre with the fringed edge higher. Curve the inner row of stamens in towards the stigma.

The Calyx

- Use a small star calyx cutter and pale green paste.

- Make a small Mexican hat shape, thin out the flat side with a cable needle. Cut out calyx, thin points with a small ball tool. Put to one side but don't allow to dry out.

The Petals

- Cut five petals from bright yellow paste, using a miniature rose petal cutter.

- Press petals against a veiner. Thin the edges with a small ball tool and cup the centre.

- Brush the sepals of the calyx with egg white, holding it at the base, lay petals evenly around slightly overlapping in a spiral with the points meeting in the centre.

- Take the wired stamens and insert the wire through the centre of the petals. Pull through firmly. Adjust petals to your own satisfaction.

- Paint dry petals with gum arabic to give a shine.

Leaves

- Follow instructions on page 8. These leaves should be made in three sections, wired with a fine wire and taped together when dry and set. See Templates on page 83.

    When using the Buttercup leaf-cutter, the leaves will not need to be made in sections.

·BUTTERCUP·

Campion, Clover & Dog Roses

The continuity of the design is enhanced by using three different techniques to produce an informal and attractive cake.

METHOD

- Cover the cake with pale mauve sugarpaste and transfer the rose design to the top.

- Pipe a neat snailstrail around the base with a N⁰.1 tube (tip). Attach a narrow band of ribbon to the cake, just above the snailstrail.

- Work the rose design on top of the cake in brush or tube embroidery. Always work from the background towards the front, leaving the most prominent features until last.

- If you choose brush embroidery as in the picture, the flowers will look more delicate if they are worked in white icing and a pale pink colouring introduced when the icing is being brushed through. Add a little piping gel to the Royal icing (approximately ½ teaspoon to 8oz icing) this will delay the drying time and allow extra time for brushing through the petals and leaves.

- Always brush in the direction of the natural veining using long strokes of a damp paintbrush.

- Pipe lace motifs with a '0' icing tube (tip) and Royal icing without glycerine, on wax paper or non-stick plastic film. When dry, lift carefully and attach in a straight line to the base of the cake with dots of icing.

- Arrange Campion and Clover, with a background of roses, in a piece of modelling paste which has been attached to the cake board. It is important that the paste foundation should be completely concealed so it must be kept small. Spare leaves are useful for covering the base.

Use a photocopier with enlarge facility to increase the size of the templates provided below.

Template.

Pattern for brush embroidery.

· CAMPION CAKE ·

Campion

The red and the white Campions look similar in appearance but they vary in some ways.

The White Campion's petals are open day and night but only at night does it produce a faint scent attracting the moths which polinate it. The five deeply notched petals have scales at the base. There are five stamens.

The Red Campion is day flowering and is pollinated by bees. The petals have smaller scales at the base, hardly noticable and five white curly stamens. It is altogether smaller than the White Campion and the flowers form clusters.

Both types have swollen bladder-like sepal tubes with five pointed teeth. When Red and White Campion grow in the same place, they will hybridise and the resulting plants will produce pink flowers.

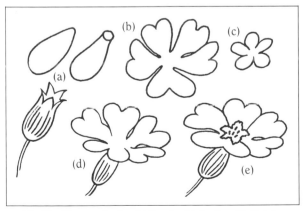

(a) Bladder-like sepal tube. (b) Petals. (c) Scales. (d) Petals centrally placed on sepal tube. (e) Finished flower.

METHOD

- Take a pea-sized ball of mid-green paste. Roll into a cone shape. Insert a cocktail stick into the pointed end and widen the hole slightly. Cut five pointed notches around the edge. Insert a 26g hooked wire into the base, keeping its rounded shape.

- Roll white paste thinly. Cut out petals with Primrose or Campion cutter. Cut a deeper notch in between each petal. Thin edges with a ball tool. Brush sepals with egg white. Place petals centrally on the sepals.

- Roll out a small piece of white paste. Cut out a very small blossom shape. Frill the edges. Place this in the centre of the flower to represent the scales at the base of the petals. Make a small hole in the centre. Insert five stamens.

- Attach two small pointed leaves opposite each other just below the flower.

- Brush one side of the bladder-like sepal tube with purple dust also the underside of the leaves.

Hazel Catkins

Hanging Catkins appear in Spring on many trees. These are the male flowers, often referred to as "lambs' tails". They make an attractive addition to an arrangement of Spring flowers.

METHOD

There are several ways to make catkins and some are quite time-consuming. The following is a quick, simple method which will produce a similar overall effect.

- Take a ball of pale greenish-yellow paste about 6mm.
- Moisten the end of a short length of cotton with egg white or gum glue.

- Hold the cotton next to the ball of paste and roll between thumb and finger to make a cigar shape about $^3/_4''$ (2cm) long.
- The cotton should now be inside the paste which should have taken the shape of a catkin.
- Insert a needle to make it easy to hold, and texture by pinching with pointed metal tweezers. Allow to dry.
- Brush the catkin lightly with egg white and roll it in a small dish containing ground maize or semolina, this will add the rough texture necessary to create the illusion of catkins covered with pollen. Make more catkins and leave to dry.
- Brush the catkins with coloured dusting powders ranging from golden yellow to brown, allowing some of the green colour to show through.
- The catkins appear before the leaves and should be arranged in pairs.
- Take a piece of 24g. wire. Make nodules by twisting the wire into knots at intervals. Start binding it with brown stem tape to make a twig.
- Brown buds on the twig can be made by cutting diagonally into the tape, twisting this into a little knot and binding it in.
- Attach a pair of catkins to the end of the twig, binding in all of the cotton and allowing them to hang freely.
- Bend the wire into a realistic twig shape, adding other twigs with catkins to make an attractive branch.

* N.B. It is useful to keep a small pot of ground maize which has yellow or brown dusting powder mixed with it.

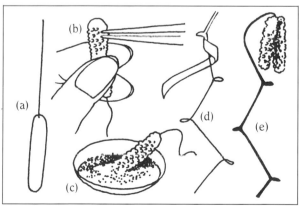

(a) Cigar-shaped paste hanging from cotton.
(b) Texturing with tweezers. (c) Rolling in maize.
(d) Binding wire. (e) Catkins attached to stem.

Red Clover

Apart from being a very pretty flower, the Clover is very useful to the farmer. It is grown for cattle fodder but also enriches the soil by converting nitrogen from the air into salts which are essential to plant growth. Its delicate scent makes it attractive to flies, butterflies and bees. The flowers are a particularly valuable source of nectar which is converted by the bees into a fragrant honey.

A member of the pea family, the rounded head is composed of many tiny florets, each one with tiny sepals of its own, these show as a hazy greenish tinge deep within the flower.

METHOD

- Take a ball of green paste approx $^3/_8''$ (1cm). Insert a hooked 28g wire into the base.
- Make florets with mauvy-pink paste. Cut out with a mini rose petal or clover cutter. If a cutter is not available, make the shape as follows. (1) Roll tiny ball of paste into a cigar shape. Flatten by pressing with cocktail stick and roll it back and forth to thin and shape. (2) Place the cocktail stick on the petal with pointed end of the stick against round edge of the petal. (3) Twist petal around point of stick and remove stick. (4) Make a small cut in the folded front edge with scissors. Push this cut section inside the main petal.
- Make about 15–20 florets. These are attached to the centre with pale green Royal icing. This will dry quicker than other 'glues'. Make small unopened florets by rolling minute pieces of paste into cigar shapes. Start with a cluster of these in the centre.
- Attach rows of flowers in icing, all standing upright, not too closely packed together. Gradually work down to the base, positioning florets so that they are between the florets of the previous row. Refer to a photograph of a completed flower or a real specimen for the position.
- The green icing showing between the florets will create the impression of the sepals at the base of the flower.
- The trefoil leaves may be made with a Clover leaf cutter or template (*see page* 8).
- Brush the completed leaves with dark green blossom tint. Paint a white 'V' on the surface of the leaves with white blossom tint mixed with spirit.
- Tape two small leaves immediately under the flower head, tape the remainder of the stem. Position larger leaves around the base of the flower.

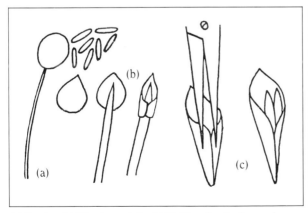

(a) Centre. (b) Shaping petals. (c) Cutting front edge and tucking inside to form inner petals.

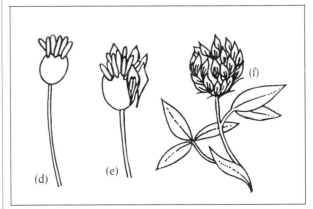

(d) Buds arranged on top of centre. (e) Open florets introduced. (f) Each row of florets positioned between those of previous row.

· CLOVER ·

Columbine

The Columbine is to be found in woods and scrubland during April and May. The wild version is usually blue but is occasionally white or pink. It is tall with nodding, five-petalled flowers. The petals are horn-shaped with the tip curled over into a spur. The oval-pointed sepals stand out between the petals and are the same colour.

METHOD

Stamens

The Columbine has many stamens (about 50) which can only be suggested rather than fully represented.

- Tape together three 26g wires about 6″ (15cm) long.
- Tape fine yellow stamens to the wires.

Petals

- Roll a ¼″ (6mm) ball of bluey-purple paste into a long tapering cone 1¼″ (3cm) long. Insert a cocktail stick into the bulbous end. Hollow (see page 6).
- Cut a V shape from one side, pinch to form a point. Curl the thin pointed base of the petals towards the centre. Make 5.
- Colour a small amount of Royal icing the same colour as the petals (or use a sticky adhesive made by mixing together gum paste with egg white).
- Pipe a bulb of icing or dab a little of the 'glue' to the base of the stamens. Attach one petal with the pointed spur curling in towards the stem. Carefully attach the other four, evenly spaced with the tops of the petals level. Allow to dry.
- Roll out paste thinly. Cut out sepals from template or with special cutter now available.
- Thin the edges of each sepal with a small ball tool. Mark a vein down the centre or vein with leaf veiner. Pinch the base of the sepal to point it. Pipe a dot of icing between the petals and firmly attach the sepals, curving them away from the centre.
- When the flower is dry and firm, carefully bend the wire until the head is hanging.

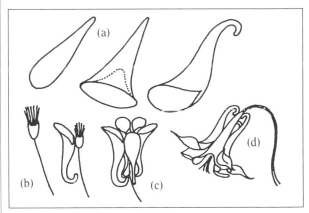

(a) Shaping of the petals. (b) Wired stamens. (c) Arranging petals around the stamens. (d) Sepals in between petals.

Cornflower

Cornflowers have become rare in the countryside due to the use of herbicides, but they can be found in a few areas June–August and they make a lovely deep blue contrast to the poppies, daisies and corn.

● **To make the stamens:** take a length of deep purple, silky embroidery thread. Wind around two fingers about eight times, making a circle. Pass a length of 30g wire through the circle, bringing the ends together, twist firmly. Cut the thread about ½″ away from the wire leaving a bushy tuft. Cut short lengths of black stamen cottons, push these in between the purple stamens. Paint the tips with white colouring (*see page* 7).

● **To make the calyx**: take a pea-sized ball of green paste. Hollow (*see page* 6).

● Cut the top edge into points with a pair of small scissors. Curve the points outward slightly. Cut small 'V'-shaped bracts around the stem with pointed scissors. Repeat until the top edge is reached. Paint a feathery black edge to each of the bracts with a fine paintbrush and black food colouring. Insert the wired centre.

● **To make the florets:** take a ball of deep blue paste about 3mm. Roll it into a long cone shape. Hollow (see page 6). Cut 7 deep V's around the edge.

● Brush the edge of the calyx with egg white. Attach the floret to the low point of the 'V'. The head of the flower should be sticking out at right-angles to the calyx. Repeat until there is a circle of flowers around the cotton centre, all attached to the low points.

● Make more florets the same way, attach these to the high points of the v's in between the florets of the first row. There should now be a double circle of florets around the edge with a mass of purple and black stamens in the centre.

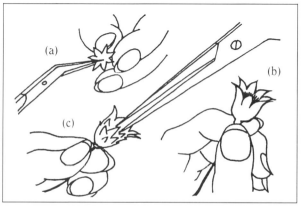

(a) Cutting pointed sepals. (b) Wired stamens pulled through calyx. (c) Cutting bracts.

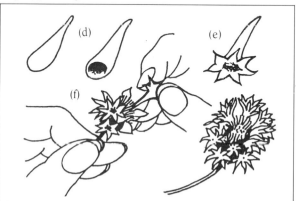

(d) Hollowed petal tube. (e) Petals. (f) Florets arranged around edge of calyx.

Apple Blossom Cake

Diagonal extension work has become a popular form of decoration for petal or round cakes. A narrow band of ribbon, a deeper pink than the cake is attached just above the extension work, this shows up the delicate white lace which overlaps it.

METHOD

- Cover an 8″ (20cm) petal cake and the board with pale pink sugarpaste. Place the extension work template against the side of the cake and prick the top and bottom guidelines. Pipe a fine snailstrail around the base with a '0' icing tube (tip). Prick out the pattern for the focal points of the embroidery. Pipe embroidery with a '00' tube (tip).

- Neatly attach a 1.5mm wide satin ribbon just above the top line of the extension work with a few dots of Royal icing.

Lace

Make lace pieces by placing the pattern under non-stick plastic film. Pipe over the pattern using a 00 tube (tip). Allow to dry thoroughly.

Extension Work

- With the cake tilted away from you, work the bridge with a '0' tube (tip) and Royal icing. Pipe a row of dropped loops, making sure they are touching the cake as gaps will cause weakness in the bridge. Pipe approximately eight rows, or however many you need to give the depth you wish to achieve. Allow each row to dry before piping over it.

- Pipe fine vertical threads from the ribbon to the bridge with a '00' tube (tip). Let out the thread and gently pull down until it is just below the bridge. When it is attached, gently clean any excess icing away from the bridge with a damp brush. Pipe threads close together. Finish by piping a dropped loop over the bridge line to neaten.

- Attach lace pieces to the top edge of the ribbon using small dots of icing.

- Tape together a spray of dainty crab apple flowers, buds and leaves. To accentuate the delicate colouring of the flowers, bind the stems with brown tape to contrast. Attach the spray to the cake by sticking a tiny piece of brownish coloured sugarpaste to the cake with gum glue or Royal icing. Lay the spray onto the cushion of paste, pressing gently to secure. Remove any excess paste and mould the remainder around the stem until it blends into the shape. Attach tiny clusters of flowers and leaves to the board. Tape the flowers together, cut the stems very short and attach them to the board with Royal icing or a cushion of paste which must be small enough to be hidden by the flowers.

N.B. For extension work and lace do not add any glycerine to your icing.

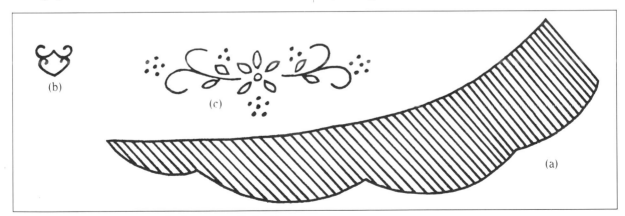

TEMPLATES: (a) Extension work. (b) Lace. (c) Embroidery.

· APPLE BLOSSOM ·

Crab Apple

The ancestor of all the cultivated apples of today. New varieties are produced by grafting onto the root stock. The small bitter fruits are popular with birds and are still made into jellies, jams and wine. Fermented crab apple juice was once used as a remedy for scalds and sprains.

The flowers are pink or white and grow in loose clusters in late Spring. This pretty delicate flower is often used with roses or other similar sized flowers on wedding cakes.

METHOD

Calyx

● Using a ball of green paste about 5mm, make a small Mexican hat shape (see page 7). Cut out with a small star calyx. Thin the points with a small ball tool. Push a 28g hooked wire into the base, neaten the back by rolling between fingers.

Petals

● Roll out white paste thinly. Cut out five petals with a miniature rose petal cutter. Thin the edges and cup the centres with a ball tool and press lightly against a petal veiner.

● Moisten the calyx with egg white or gum glue, arrange the petals overlapping with the points meeting at the centre.

● Pipe a dot of royal icing in the centre, insert approximately 10 short fine yellow stamens. Allow to dry.

Buds

● Make calyx as before. Roll a very small ball of white paste. Make five cuts across the top of the bud to represent divisions between the petals. Attach to the calyx with egg white.

● Draw sepals up around the bud.

● Dust the edges of the petals, the backs of the flowers and the buds with pink dusting powder.

● Make pointed oval leaves.

● To arrange naturally, tape a few buds and flowers together, arrange 2-3 leaves immediately below to form a cluster.

● When forming a bough, the bound stem should be dusted with a little brown or black in places to give the appearance of wood.

Cyclamen

Wild cyclamen flowers August–September in woodlands. It is found mainly in the South of England and is quite uncommon. The wild cyclamen is generally smaller than the cultivated version and is pink with purple shading at the base of the turned-back petals. There are two small lobes at the base of each petal.

METHOD

- Take a pea-sized ball of white paste, roll into a cone. Hollow by pushing a pointed ball tool into the wide end. Insert a hooked piece of 24g wire into the base. Neaten the back by rolling between fingers. Leave to set. Make a small calyx. Attach to the base of the cone with gum glue or egg white.
- Cut five petals with a cutter or template. Thin the edges with a ball tool, press against a veiner to texture. Tool the centre of the petals lightly to curve, leaving the straight base flat, give a twist to the petals and leave to set a little, this will allow you to assemble the petals with plenty of movement.
- Moisten the flat base of the petal with egg white or gum paste glue, attach petal to the cone with the base level with the rim of the cone and the petal hanging down
- Attach four more petals around rim of the cone.
- When all the petals are firmly attached, pinch two small lobes at the base of each petal with tweezers.

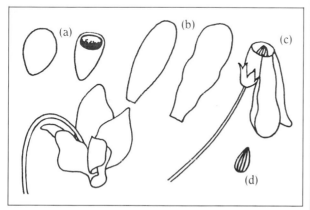

(a) Hollowed cone. (b) Cut and shaped petals. (c) Petals arranged on central cone. (d) Stamen cluster.

- Before the petals are completely dry, turn the flower upright and adjust the position of the petals if necessary. Press a tiny cone of paste into the hollow of the central cone and mark five lines with a knife blade (This is to represent 5 stamens which form a cone) Paint a dark greyish green.
- Dust the flowers in various shades of pink. Paint the base of the petals purple.
- The stem is a brownish-pink in colour and very fleshy. To obtain this effect, moisten the wire with egg white. Roll a small piece of suitably coloured paste around the wire. As you roll between your fingers the paste will travel up the wire.
- Bend the stem by gripping with tweezers just below the base of the flower while the paste is still soft. The head of the flower should now be hanging with the petals standing upright.
- Make heart shaped leaves also with fleshy stems. The leaves are dark green, often with pale marks following the shape of the leaf, within the edge.
- Buds are long and narrow. Roll the paste into a cigar shape about $^3/_8''$ (1cm). Insert a hooked wire. Attach a small calyx cut with a small star.

Dog Rose

One of the most beautiful of wild flowers, abounding in the hedgerows and adorning them with its delicately scented shell-pink flowers. One explanation of its unflattering name goes back to the ancient Greeks, who called the wild rose 'dog rose' because they believed that its roots could cure a man bitten by a mad dog.

METHOD

The Bud

Roll a 5mm ball of green paste into a small cone. Insert a hooked 24g wire into the base and secure with egg white. Make the calyx as follows. Take a ball of green paste approximately 1cm. Make a Mexican hat shape (see page 7). Cut out shape with a rose calyx cutter. Thin the edges with a ball tool. Snip the sepals at intervals with small scissors. Slip the wired bud through the centre of the sepals, drawing them up to completely cover the bud. Roll base between fingers to attain the rose-hip shape. Remove any excess paste.

The Flower

Make the calyx as for the bud. Push a hooked 24g wire through the centre of the calyx and neaten the back. Cut out five petals with dog rose cutter. Thin edges and cup with a ball tool. Press petals on a veiner. Brush sepals with gum glue and arrange petals with points to the centre (Refer to numbered diagram for order of assembly).

Although the petals overlap they do not form a complete spiral. There will always be one petal overlapped on both sides and the last petal lying on top of all the others. If using ready-made fine stamens, make a tiny pale yellow cone. Brush the top with gum glue and dip into ground maize, coloured yellowy-green. Attach to the centre of the flower using egg white or gum glue. Cut many short stamens. Stick these stamens into the residue of glue around the edge of the centre. Stipple a little yellow and brown colour on the tips of the stamens.

Cotton stamens

These make a very effective alternative centre when a flower such as this has masses of stamens. Use cream-coloured fine sewing thread and make as for the centre of the Cornflower, sticking a tiny pale green cone into the middle of the cut stamens. Moisten the tips and dip into yellow-coloured ground maize. In this case, do not wire the flower until the end, when the wired stamens are pushed into the centre of the petals.

Leaves

Make leaves by cutting out with a serrated rose leaf cutter. Vein with veiner made from real leaf (See pages 8–9). At the base of the leaf stem are a pair of stipules which can be made from paste and attached to the stem after binding. (see diagram). Brush leaves with gum arabic glaze to obtain a sheen. Tape groups of five leaves together. Tape clusters of flowers, leaves and buds together.

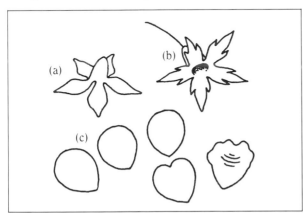

(a) Calyx. (b) Shaped calyx. (c) Petals shaped and fluted.

Positions for leaves and petals.

·DOG ROSE·

Rose and Speedwell Wedding Cake

Dog Roses and Speedwell form the theme of this Summer Wedding Cake. The lace filigree motifs have the same flowers embroidered in them. This cake is for the experienced decorator.

METHOD

Filigree Motifs

You will need six filigree motifs for each cake. Make several extra pieces to allow for breakages.

- Trace the pattern and place under a piece of non-stick plastic film. Pipe all the outlines using fresh Royal icing and a 00 tube (tip). Do not use colours containing glycerol for this work as it will soften the icing.

- The pattern for the bridgeless extension work must be drawn accurately so that the pieces fit, otherwise sections could become stressed and this will cause breakages.

- Draw a line on a large piece of paper the exact length of the diameter of the cake. Mark the centre. Using a pair of compasses with the point to the centre draw a circle the exact size of the cake. Draw an outer circle leaving $1/2''$ (1.25cm) clearance between circles. Use a protractor to mark off six sections of 60° around the circle.

- Make a paper template exactly the measurement of the sides of the cake. Fold into six sections. Trace the outline of the motifs centrally over the folds of the template. Draw a guideline for the top of the extension work on one section and trace through to the other sections.

- Draw a second line showing where the bridge will be (this is for reference to show the position and should be about $1^1/4''$ (3cm) away from the top line). Do not mark this line on the cake.

- Wrap the template around the cake and secure with sticky tape. Make a pinprick at each fold to mark the position of the filigree motifs. Mark the top of the extension work by pricking through the guideline on to the cake.

- Before starting any of the delicate work, pipe a neat band of embroidery all around the cake, just above the top line of the extension work.

The Bridge

- Cut out one section of the bridge pattern and use the outer line as a guide for piping the bridge. Place the pattern under a piece of non-stick film. Pipe over the line with a 0 tube (tip) and white Royal icing. Pipe another line exactly on top. You will need six but pipe extra in case of breakages.

- Attach the motifs to the cake, in the positions marked, with dots of Royal icing, securing firmly. Support the bottom of each motif so that each one is $1/2''$ (1.25cm) away from the cake. Leave to dry.

- Remove each section of bridge from the plastic film with a thin-bladed palette knife and carefully lift into position between the lace motifs. Support on blocks or with 'L' brackets. Attach to the side edges of the lace motifs with dots of icing. Repeat with the other sections of the bridge.

- Pipe a few stabilising threads from the top guideline to the bridge. When these are dry, the blocks or brackets may be removed.

- Pipe fine curtainwork with a 00 tube (tip) all around the cake, attaching the threads neatly when piping around the filigree motifs.

- Finish the edge either by piping decorative loops or dots along the bridge OR Remove the bridge as follows:
  – Pipe a row of dots between alternate threads of curtain work, just above the bridge, joining pairs together. Damp the bridge very carefully with a wet paintbrush working on a small section at a time until it separates from the extension work. Seal each short section at once by piping another row of dots underneath and between the dots of the first row.
  – Take care not to knock and dislodge filigree motifs when separating them from the bridge.
  – Pipe a fine snailstrail to neaten the top of the extension work.

Templates for this cake can be found on page 84.

* NOTE: 'L' Brackets (see details in acknowledgements at the front of the book) or blocks are required to support the floating extension work. When using 'L' Brackets it will be necessary to place the cake and board on a second board of the same size. The brackets are fixed in between.

· ROSE & SPEEDWELL ·

Field Mouse Ear

This pretty white flower blooms April–August in dry open places. The connection with mice is not obvious until touching the plants. All have short downy hairs on the leaves like those on the ears of a mouse. It has five notched petals and fine yellow stamens, with pale green shading in the centre. The delicate colouring makes it a very good filler flower, blending well with many colour schemes.

METHOD

- Use a medium size Primrose cutter for the petals and small star for the calyx.

- Take a small ball of pale green paste about 6mm. Make a Mexican hat shape (see page 7). Place star calyx cutter over the central knob and cut out. Thin points of the calyx by stroking with a small ball tool.

- Insert hooked 28g wire moistened with egg white through the centre.

- Cut petals from thinly rolled white paste using a Primrose cutter. Cut the divisions between the petals a bit deeper towards the centre. Soften the edges of the petals by stroking with a ball tool.

- Thin the petals more by rolling a cocktail stick back and forth across each one.

- Brush the sepals of the calyx with egg white. Lay the petals centrally on calyx. Push a pointed ball tool into the centre making a small hole. Insert ten fine yellow stamens. (If you have to use coarser stamens you should use less than ten to get a similar effect).

- The stems usually have a flower, with a few buds slightly lower and pairs of small pointed leaves at intervals on opposite sides of the stem.

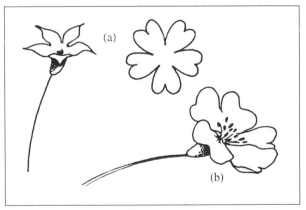

(a) Calyx and cut petals. (b) Flower complete with stamens.

Forget-me-not

Legend has it that the forget-me-not acquired its name from the plight of a medieval knight who picked a bunch of these flowers for his lady while they were walking on the river bank. He over-balanced and fell into the river and the heavy armour pulled him under the water. As he was drowning he threw the flowers to the lady crying 'forget me not'. Whether the story is true or false, the flower has, since the Middle Ages, been associated with love and was worn to ensure that a lover remained faithful.

Herbalists recommended forget-me-not syrup as a cure for coughs and lung ailments. It blooms from April–September in woods and hedges, a pretty little blue flower with a yellow eye. The tip of the stem is curled but straightens as the buds open. The flowers are very small and grow in spikes.

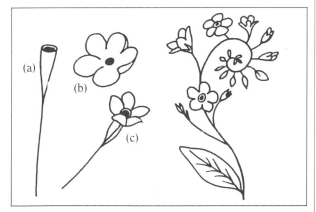

(a) Hollow flower centre. (b) Shaped petals. (c) Petals attached to centre.

METHOD

- **To make centre:** Take a tiny ball of yellow paste about 2mm. Roll into a cigar-shape and hollow with a cocktail stick. Insert a stamen or very fine short wire through the central hole.

- **To make petals:** Roll out white paste very thin. Cut out the shape with the smallest blossom cutter. Soften the edges of the petals with a small ball tool or glass-headed pin.

- Make a hole in the centre with a cocktail stick. Moisten the yellow centre with egg white. Push wire through the centre of the petals and pull through until only a yellow ring remains in view.

- When dry, brush the petals with blue, leaving a little white showing around the yellow centre.

- **To make calyx:** Paint the central yellow cone at the base of the flower with green food colouring, ending with five small points around the base of each flower.

- Make 5–7 flowers for each spike. Make many tiny pinkish coloured buds from paste and stick to the end of the wire. Alternatively pipe the buds with a No. l icing tube. Dry well.

- Bind flowers to the central wire with stem tape. Gently curl over the tip of the stem.

Filigree Forget-me-not Cake

This filigree cake has a top ornament of Wood Anemones with Forget-me-nots. The pink shading on the backs of the Wood Anemones adds warmth to the blue which can look cold by itself.

METHOD

Panels for a cake of this type must be mathematically correct and this design will fit an 8″ (20cm) round cake. The panels could also be used on a hexagonal cake.

- Cover the cake and board with two coats of Royal icing. Leave to dry.

- Draw a circle larger than the cake, leaving ¹/₂″ (1.25cm) clearance all round. Use a protractor to mark off six equal divisions in the circle. Measure the distance between marks and this will be the width of the panels. The height will be ¹/₂″ (1.25cm) more than the cake.

- Mark a line on the board, exactly ¹/₂″ (1.25cm) away from the cake.

- Place the pattern for the panel under non-stick plastic film. Pipe the filigree with fresh Royal icing mixed by hand, or, if using an electric mixer on its slowest speed, allow to stand over night for the icing to relax and any bubbles to break down.

- Use a '0' tube (tip) for leaves and flowers. Use a '1' for the main stems, this will add interest to the panel by varying the textures. The lattice border is piped with a '0'. Solid borders either side of the lattice-work are piped with a '0' and flooded with icing let down to runout consistency by the addition of water or albumen. If the consistency is correct, any trails of icing dribbled onto the surface should disappear at the count of 10. Make six panels.

- Pipe a collar using a '0' tube (tip) for the filigree insets and '1' for outlining all of the collar. Half fill a large parchment piping bag, without an icing tube (tip) with runout icing. Cut a small hole in the tip of the bag the size of a N⁰.2 tube. Flood the collar carefully, pricking any bubbles which rise to the surface. Work a small area at a time, working from side to side of the flooding to prevent a line forming between soft and dry icing. Allow to dry in a warm place or under a lamp to give a good sheen to the icing. When quite dry, pipe dots around the collar to form a picot edge.

- Remove the filigree panels from the plastic film and attach each one, positioning the centre of the panel on the line. Support with a block until dry. Pipe a line of icing down the side and the bottom of the second panel and butt this up against the first, still keeping the centre on the line. Repeat until all the panels are in place. These will be a good fit if the measurements are accurate.

- Pipe a line of icing around the top edge of the panels. Carefully lower the collar into position, matching points.

- Pipe extension lines to the inside edge of the collar, drawing them up from the top of the cake to the inside edge of the collar.

Templates

To enlarge these templates to the correct size use a photocopier with enlarge facility.

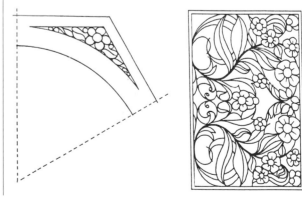

NOTE: Filigree can be quite strong if piped correctly. Make sure that each line touches another at some point. Failure to do this will result in weak spots and breakages could occur.

· CYNTHIA VENN ·

·FILIGREE CAKE·

Harebell

The dainty pale blue bells of the harebell dance in the breeze on their fine stems. These are the 'bluebells of Scotland' although they are actually unrelated to the bluebell. They flower July–September and are commonly found on dry grassy banks.

The narrow green bracts which grow at the base of each flower stem get larger towards the bottom of the main stem and become more oval and toothed. The plant also produces heart-shaped leaves at the base but these have not been shown since they usually die off before the flowers appear.

METHOD

- Make a hook in the end of a 28–30g wire. Make a Mexican hat (see page 7). Cut out the shape with cutter (a).
- Hollow the centre by pushing a small balling tool deep into it, this will also make the base rounded. Lay flower on its side and thin each point by rolling lightly with a cocktail stick or knitting needle.

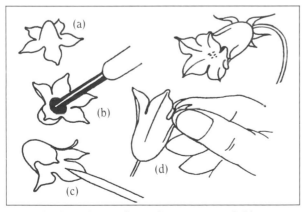

(a) Petals. (b) Hollowing flower, keeping a rounded base.
(c) Thinning petals. (d) Pinching a crease in centre of petals.

- Pinch each point to make a sharp crease down the length of each petal. If the flower begins to lose the rounded shape at the base, push the ball tool into it again to reform.
- Push hooked wire through the centre of the flower, curl back the points of the petals. Press a tiny ball of blue paste into the centre to hold the stamens and secure the wire. Insert five very fine stamens deep into the flower tube.
- Cut a calyx with thinly rolled green paste and the smaller star shaped cutter (b). Pinch and roll each point between thumb and finger until they are long and thin. Brush the base of the flower with egg white and slide calyx over the wire and on to the flower. Pinch and roll the base of the calyx between fingers to form the ovary. Curve points away from the flower. Grasp stem firmly just underneath the flower with tweezers and bend flower over.
- Make buds by rolling a small ball of paste into a cigar shape, push hooked wire through the base. Attach calyx as for flower. Tape stems with green stem tape and assemble buds and two to three flowers well-spaced along the stem. Cut small, thin lance-shaped leaves and stick them with egg white to the base of the stem of each flower. Add progressively larger leaves lower down the stem.

Honeysuckle

This sweet smelling climber is common in woods and hedgerows June–September. The creamy coloured flowers are often tinged with peachy-red at the base. Its scent is stronger in the evening, which prompted Samuel Pepys to call it 'the trumpet flower whose bugles blow scent instead of sound'. There is an old superstition that if it is brought into the house a wedding will follow. What could be more suitable for a wedding or engagement cake? The flowers and buds should be kept small and dainty.

METHOD

- **To make stamens:** tape five very fine short stamens and one long (for stigma) to a piece of 30g wire. The easiest way to do this is to start taping from about midway along the wire towards the tip, stop about $1/2''$ (1.25cm) from the end.

- Hold stamens against the wire and continue taping, enclosing them at the same time. (Cotton stamens made by method shown for Dog Rose are also very effective.)

- Roll a small ball of paste approx $1/4''$ (6mm) into a cigar shape about $3/4''$ (2cm) long. Push a cocktail stick into one end until it is about half way down the tube. Hollow (*see* p.6).

- With small pointed scissors, make two long cuts very close together to make a long narrow petal. Pull this petal gently forward to separate it from the remainder.

- Open out the rest of the cylinder and cut a deep wedge from either side. Cut three small V's along the top of this broad lip, forming four lobes. Pinch between thumb and finger and gently curl back.

- Trim square corners from the narrow petal. Pinch and gently curve down towards the base. Push wired stamens through the throat and out of the bottom of the long tube. Roll the base between fingers to taper well.

- **To make buds:** Roll a smaller piece of paste into a long tapering cone. Push the wire into the base, taper the tip and narrow the base. Curve slightly over the pad of a thumb. Dust base of flowers and buds with pale orangey-red.

- Assemble buds and flowers, with cluster of buds in the centre, surrounded by flowers. The flowers should lie at 90° to centre buds with the long narrow petal facing downwards.

- The sepals of these flowers are very small and joined at the base. These can be represented by pressing tiny balls of green paste in between the bases of all flowers and buds, moulding into shape with a modelling tool.

- Make leaves in three sizes using cutter or template. For assembly, refer to picture.

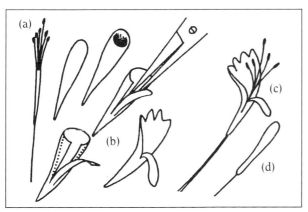

(a) Wired stamens. (b) Cutting petals. (c) Stamens pulled through centre of flower. (d) Bud.

Honeysuckle Wedding Cake

Honeysuckle is a popular choice for brides and it is displayed on this cake, trailing naturally, without the addition of any other flowers. This is to accentuate the attractive trailing habit of the leaf stems and the delicate colouring of the flowers.

Another climber, White Bryony, is shown decorating the Spiral Stand. The only decoration apart from the moulded flowers is the embroidery which is entirely composed of two small honeysuckle motifs.

METHOD

- The cakes and boards were covered with a soft peach-coloured sugar paste. Colours used were paprika (or flesh tone) and just a touch of yellow.

- For the embroidered circular borders, draw a circle 2″ (5cm) less in diameter than the top of the cake. Fold the template into four. Trace off the pairs of honeysuckle motifs, placing one at each fold of the template, around the circle. Space the other motifs in between.

- Allow the icing to harden for a few days before transferring the design.

- Place a template on the cake and prick or scribe an impression on to the cake.

- Make a template exactly the same size as the sides of the cake. Trace single, regularly spaced motifs. Scribe onto the cake.

- Embroider flowers and leaves with Royal icing and a '0' icing tube (tip). The petals and leaves are worked with tiny short lines as in satin stitch.

- Make up clusters of honeysuckle flowers and buds and tape these into a long stem interspersed with leaves, add short stems of small leaves here and there without flowers before arranging on the cakes naturally.

- Tape several stems together, bend into a pleasing shape which fits the contours of the cake. Insert a small plastic posy holder into the side of the cake after carefully marking the correct place. Push a small piece of soft paste into the holder and set the stems in place. Prop them in position until the paste has dried hard enough to support them. Single leaves are useful for disguising the plastic holder.

- Wires should never be pushed directly into cakes

Templates

· CYNTHIA VENN ·

·HONEYSUCKLE CAKE·

The Hop

The hop climbs through hedges in most parts of the British Isles and the rest of Europe. It has been used since the Middle Ages to clarify and flavour beer. Long before it was cultivated commercially, farmers and innkeepers kept their own small hop gardens to flavour their homemade brews. Hops are considered to be a good sedative and herbal pillows containing hops are recommended to combat insomnia. The plant spirals round other stems, always in a clockwise manner. A cone of pale green papery scales encloses the nut-like fruit and it is the female fruit which is harvested. The hop looks very attractive on cakes where a trailing effect is required.

METHOD

The Hops

- Make a hook in the end of a 28g wire. Attach a 3mm ball of pale green paste.

- Make the bracts with small and medium size 5-lobe calyx cutters or special hop cutters. Roll out the paste very thin and cut three small calyx shapes and two medium. (cover the four spare ones with plastic film while working on the first one).

- Thin out the bracts by smoothing with a ball tool. Curve by stroking with a ball tool from the tip towards the centre. Moisten the paste on the wire. Thread the bracts onto the wire and close the points over the central core.

- Repeat with a second small shape but before sliding onto the wire, thread on a tiny bead of paste to act as a spacer and stick to the underside of the first row of bracts. Thread on the second layer and curve it towards the first layer leaving plenty of air space between. Now treat the two medium bracts the same way and assemble with spacers as before. Finish with a small calyx shape. The finished shape of the hop should resemble a fir cone.

Leaves

- The hop has leaves with distinctive veining. For complete accuracy a latex mould can be made of a real leaf (See page 9). Some leaf cutters are quite near the shape and can be adapted by working the leaf shape with a ball tool and using scissors if necessary, or it can be cut from the template.

- Assemble hops and leaves in a long trail as shown. They can also be used individually in an Autumn arrangement if desired.

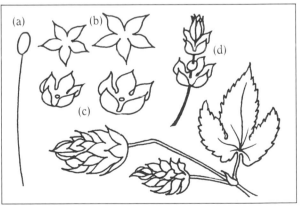

(a) Centre. (b) Small calyx shapes which form the scales. (c) Shaped scales. (d) Scales with spacers.

Ivy-Leaved Toadflax

This charming plant with its tiny mauve snapdragon-like flowers and ivy-shaped glossy leaves grows on old walls throughout Britain but it originated in Mediterranean countries. It first made an appearance in the 17th Century and it is thought that the plant was introduced by means of seeds wedged into the cracks of marble imported from Italy. The flowers grow on long stalks and stand clear of the foliage so that they are visible to the bees which pollinate them, they also have a yellow honey-guide on the lower petals to guide the insects. After fertilisation when the fruit has formed, the stem has the curious habit of curving round to allow the seed capsule to be pushed into the cracks of the wall. When the seeds are released, some germinate in the cracks to ensure continuous wall cover. It flowers May–September.

METHOD

- Make a cone shape from a tiny ball of white paste, about ¼″ (5mm). Hollow out using a cocktail stick.

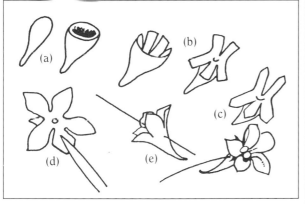

(a) Hollowed cone. (b) Petals. (c) Petal edges, shaped. (d) Thinning petal. (e) Wire emerging above the spur.

- Make three cuts at the edge of the hollow tube to form two small petals. Cut a bit deeper either side of the petals and trim a thin wedge from each side to give a greater division between the top petals and the bottom. Now cut the remainder of the cylinder into three sections. Round off the square edges by trimming with small pointed scissors.

- Lay the flower on its side and thin the petals by rolling them back and forth with a cocktail stick.

- Push a hooked 30g wire through the throat of the flower and exit at the top just above the little pointed tail. Curve back the petals. Pinch the sides of the flower between thumb and finger to bring the petals closer together. If the flower is to be dusted with violet powder, it should be done at this stage as soon as the flower is dry.

- Finally, the honey guide is made by rolling two very tiny balls of yellow paste. Brush throat of the flower with egg white and attach the yellow balls close together.

- **Make calyx** by hollowing a tiny cone of green paste, and snip into five sections. Pinch them into fine points. Push the wire through the centre and slide onto the flower, sticking with egg white or gum glue and moulding it around the base of the stem wire. Pinch off any surplus paste from the base of the calyx.

- **Make leaves** in pale green, cutting with small ivy-shaped cutters or templates in two or three sizes.

- Assemble by taping together the leaves, starting with the smallest, and alternating either side of the stem. Tape in flowers from the base of each leaf. Leave long stems on the flowers so they will stand higher than the leaves when taped together.

Mallow & Bryony

COMMON MALLOW

The Common Mallow has large, five-petalled pink flowers and belongs to the same family as the Holyhock and the Hibiscus. The petals have distinctive purple-red veins. They have many stamens forming a club-shaped head frequently the same colour as the petal veins, with a sprinkling of white pollen at the tips. This plant was prized as far back in history as the 8th Century BC for its value as a food and medicine. It was used as an aphrodisiac in medieval times and is still used in poultices and soothing ointments.

Its size makes it a very useful flower for cake decoration and it mixes well with smaller flowers such as White Bryony as shown here.

METHOD
- Make a Mexican hat (see page 7) with green paste. Cut out shape with small five-pointed calyx cutter. Thin the edges with a small ball tool. Moisten a 26g hooked wire and push through the calyx.

- Roll out pale pink paste very thinly. Cut out petals with a large primrose cutter. Cut a small 'V' shape between the petals to extend the division towards the centre and narrow the base of the petals. Thin the edges of the petals with a ball tool. Special Mallow cutters are now available.

- Moisten the calyx with egg white. Lay the petals centrally on the calyx.

- Make a small hole in the centre.

- Make the club-shaped cluster of stamens by rolling out a tiny ball of pink paste as shown. Stick this into the central hole with egg white. Leave to dry.

- Paint fine veins on petals with dark red food colouring, also brush a little of the same colour on the club-like centre.

- Moisten this central column with egg white, sprinkle the stamen cluster with a little ground maize or white sugartex.

- Make **half-open flowers** the same way. Draw the petals together, hang upside down until set.

WHITE BRYONY

White Bryony climbs through hedgerows by means of curling tendrils. It has large leaves and clusters of whitish green five-petalled flowers with a fine green stripe on the petals, and five bright yellow stamens in pairs. It is very attractive in Autumn when it bears green and red berries which are very poisonous. It is a useful plant for cake decorators where a trailing effect is required and its subtle colours blend well with most colour schemes.

METHOD
- Make **flowers** by making a Mexican hat with very pale green paste, cut out the flower with a small 5-pointed calyx cutter. Thin the edge of the petals with a small ball tool. Make a hollow in the centre of the flower with the end of a paintbrush or knitting needle. Insert a hooked 30g wire. Neaten the back of the flower which should be small and dainty.

- **Buds** are small and flat with five ridges at the edge.

- Make leaves using template on pages 83–4

- Make tendrils by covering fine wire with green tape and curling it around a pencil.

- To **assemble**, start with a cluster of buds and tape two small leaves to cup them. Tape down the main stem leaving plenty of space between leaves and flowers. The leaves should be taped alternately on either side of the stem with tendrils and groups of flowers at intervals.

- Long trails of Bryony make an attractive alternative to ivy for decorating cakestands or to form the base of garlands.

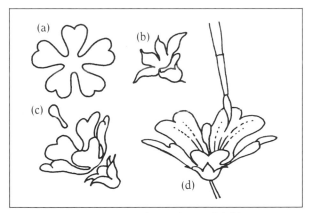

COMMON MALLOW. (a) & (b) Petals. (c) Club-like centre. (d) Painting veins.

· MALLOW & BRYONY ·

Mallow and Hops Cake

The contrast of fine extension work with the boldness of large Mallow flowers produces a well-balanced design.

METHOD

- Place the extension work template against each of the corners of the cake and mark the outer edge and the bridge lines.

- Mark the main guideline for the line-work on top of the cake.

- Pipe a snailstrail around the base with a '0' tube (tip). Attach a narrow band of satin ribbon above the snailstrail.

- Pipe the bridge for the first tier of extension work with Royal icing and a '0' or '1' tube (tip).

- Starting at one of the high points of the scalloped bridge line, pipe a line of dropped loops, this is the first row of the bridge. Pipe another line exactly on top of the first, allowing each row to dry before piping another, and continue for about 8 rows or until the bridge is deep enough. This stage is easier if the cake is slightly tilted away from you.

- To pipe the vertical strings of curtain work, using sieved Royal icing and a '0' or '00' tube (tip).

- Half fill a small parchment bag with icing. Touch the tube (tip) to the upper guideline and let out a thread of icing. Keeping the pressure even, gently pull the thread straight and attach it to the bridge. Keep the bridge clean by carefully removing any excess icing with a damp brush. Pipe the threads neatly and close together.

- Pipe the upper bridge on the marked line, above the bottom tier of extension work and proceed as for the first tier.

- Finish off the bridge line with a neat row of dots or loops. Attach lace pieces to the top edges.

- To pipe the linework border on the top of the cake. Pipe the first lines with a No. 2 tube (tip) and white Royal icing. Overpipe the first line with a N⁰·1 tube and pipe another line by the side. Pipe over all lines using contrasting icing and a '0' tube and pipe another line by the side. The border now consists of three lines, one treble, one double, and one single line.

- Attach lace to the outside edge of the border.

- Arrange groups of mallow, hops and leaves at the sides of the cake.

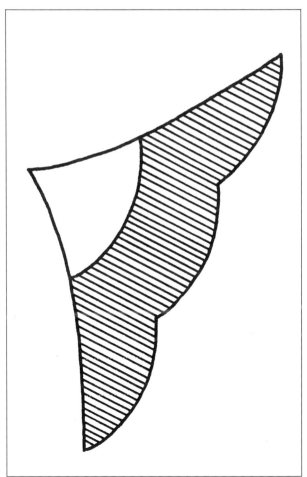

Template for extension work (actual size).

Meadow Cranesbill

A beautiful plant which grows in meadows and wayside verges from June–September. A soft violet colour with five prominent veined petals. The leaves are in groups of 3–7 irregular toothed lobes which radiate from the stem. The flower has ten black-tipped stamens and five stigmas which appear to be joined in a slender beak (hence the name Cranesbill) which separates at the tip.

METHOD

- Make a Mexican hat (page 7) with green paste. Cut out with small star calyx cutter. Thin sepals with small ball tool.

- To make **flower centre**, tape five short lengths of green cotton or fine stamen threads to a 26g wire. Dab a little egg white or gum glue on the cottons to join them together, leaving the tips free to curl outwards. This forms the stigma.

Tape ten fine stamens around the stigma. Colour the tips black.

- To make **petals**, roll out white paste very thin. Cut five petals with cutter or template. Thin the edges of the petals, press each one against a fine veiner, and cup the centres by working them with a small ball tool. Crease each petal down the centre by pinching lightly at the back. Brush the calyx with egg white and lay on the petals, overlapping with points to the centre. Push the wired stamens through the centre of the flower while the calyx is still soft, neaten the base of the calyx and trim off any excess.

- When the flower is dry, dust with pink blossom tint to pick up the veining, then dust over the top with blue-violet.

- **Make Buds** small, green, oval-shaped, pointed at the tip. Insert fine wire.

- Mark lines down the length to represent the divisions between the sepals. Tape a cluster of 3-4 buds together to form a stem. Attach this to the main flower stem.

- The plant has pointed papery-looking stipules growing beneath the buds and flowers, these are often russet coloured. Cut these from stem tape and attach to the stem.

- **Leaves** are complicated shapes and should be made in sections, individually wired. Make each leaf section referring to special instructions (page 8). Insert fine wires. Vein if possible with a veiner made from a real leaf. When the leaf sections are dry, tape them together. Arrange, radiating out from the base of the flower stem.

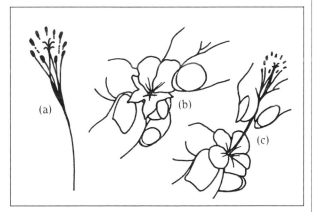

(a) Wired stamens. (b) Arranging petals on calyx. (c) Pushing stamens through centre of flower.

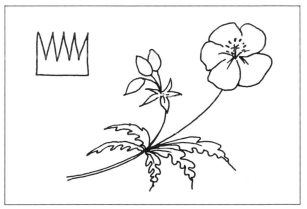

Flower and buds with reddish papery-looking stipules at the junction of the stem.

· MEADOW CRANESBILL ·

Ox-Eye Daisy

Throughout the Summer the Ox-Eye Daisy transforms mile after mile of meadows, roadsides and railway embankments into waving carpets of white and gold. It is also known as the 'Marguerite' or 'Moon Daisy' and is tall with large, solitary flower heads which can be up to 2" (50cm) in diameter. In the past, the juice from the stem was used as drops for runny eyes. An extract from the plant was used in ointments and medicines for a variety of ailments. The flower heads have an outer ring of white petals surrounding a central golden button of tiny disc florets. Beneath the flower head are rows of green bracts.

METHOD

- **To make petals:** a large size daisy cutter is needed for the outer petals and a small one for the bracts at the base.

- Make a Mexican hat with a pea-sized ball of white paste (page 7).

- Cut out the shape with a large daisy cutter. Cut each petal in half lengthwise with small scissors or a knife. Place the flower face down on a board and roll the cocktail stick back and forth to thin the petals. Press a ball tool into the centre to make a hollow.

- Make a hook in a piece of 26g covered wire, push the hook into the base of the flower, neaten the back by rolling it between your fingers. Keep it small as this is a fairly flat flower.

- Roll out a little white paste very thinly, cut another daisy shape, this time flat. Cut each petal in half and roll with a cocktail stick as for the first petals.

- Brush the centre of the first petals with egg white. Lay the second row centrally on top.

- Make a golden centre by pressing a small ball of gold coloured paste into a piece of fine mesh or a sieve to texture it. If you press well into the mesh, the paste will take on the appearance of a mass of tiny florets. Moisten the centre of the daisy with egg white and press the golden centre into the hollow. Brush the centre with egg white and dust with yellow cornmeal to make pollen. Gently tease the petals into a natural random formation.

- **To Make the Calyx:** roll out some mid-green paste.

- Cut out two shapes with a small or medium daisy cutter. Cut each lobe in half lengthwise. Thin the points. If they are too wide, trim them with scissors.

- Brush the base of the flower with egg white. Slide the bracts over the wire and stick to the base of the flower. Attach a second row of bracts, arrange beneath and lower than first row.

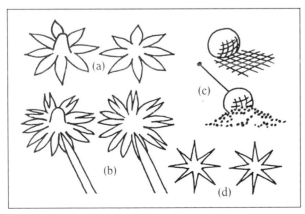

(a) Petals – two rows. (b) Splitting and shaping petals. (c) Texturing centre. (d) Calyx which forms two rows of bracts.

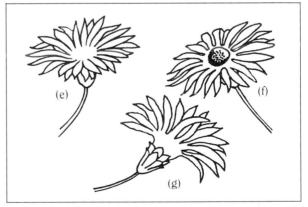

(e) Two rows of petals (f) Petals with yellow centre. (g) Double row of bracts added.

·OX EYE DAISY·

Lazy Daisy Wedding Cake

Large moulded Ox-Eye Daisies and Ivy-leaved Toadflax blend well with plentiful green leaves to promote the natural theme of this simple wedding cake. The embroidered chains of daisies and leaves continue the design around the sides of the cakes.

The border design of daisies can be used as a whole or you could trace off sections and re-group them as you please.

- Transfer the embroidery design to the cake by tracing on to a greaseproof paper template the exact size of the cake. The design is slightly larger and more prominent in one section, this should be placed at the front of the cake, graduating to a smaller design at the back.

- Prick through the main points of the design with a pin or scriber, the remaining pattern can then easily be piped freehand.

- The tube embroidery is executed with Royal icing and a No.0 tube (tip). The flowers are worked by piping a series of short straight lines in the direction of the natural veining of the petal or leaf. If the result is a little uneven it can be smoothed by gently stroking with a damp paintbrush. This is also useful for blending different shades of icing.

- Arrange natural looking posies of Ox-Eye Daisies and Ivy-leaved Toadflax. Stick these to the cake by inserting a plastic posy holder into the cake and pushing in the wires. These can be secured by putting a little Royal icing or soft modelling paste at the bottom of the holder.

- Templates for brush embroidery may be enlarged by using a photocopier with enlarge facility set to 200 percent.

·LAZY DAISY CAKE·

Lesser Periwinkle

An evergreen – carpeting shady banksides with glossy leaves and violet-blue white-centred blooms. One of the earliest Spring flowers February–May. In medieval England, crowns of Periwinkles were sometimes worn by people about to be executed, probably because the evergreen plant was considered to be a symbol of immortality. It was used as a fertility aid and was also thought to stop nose-bleeds when hung around the neck in a garland.

METHOD

The easiest way to achieve the white centre is to make the flower white and dust when dry with violet-blue dust.

- Take a pea-sized ball of white paste and roll it into a cone-shape.

- Hollow and widen (see page 6). Make five evenly spaced deep cuts with a pair of small pointed scissors.

- Round off the square edges of the petals and trim at an angle so that the right side is slightly longer than the left.

- Make a hole in the centre of the flower to form a throat, this has five square edges.

- Thin the edges of the petals and slightly cup the centres with a ball tool. Vein the petals.

- Insert a 28g hooked wire into the base and thin the back by rolling between fingers.

- Place a yellow stamen in the centre to represent the stigma. The stamens are inside the petal tube and are not visible.

- When dry carefully brush the back and front of the petals with blue dust, leaving a white area in the centre. This can be made easier by masking the centre with a small piece of soft paste which is removed after the dusting has been completed.

- If you wish to use a cutter for the petals, make a Mexican Hat (see page 7) and after cutting out, refer to main instructions.

- Make a **calyx** with green paste. Roll out paste thinly, cut shape with a small star calyx cutter. Pinch the calyx points to narrow them. Slip over the wire and attach to the base of the flower with egg white.

- Make buds. Roll a ball of paste one-quarter the size of the flower into a cigar shape. Roll the tip into a point. Insert hooked wire into the base. Add small calyx.

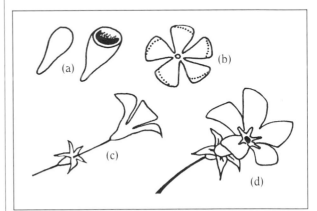

(a) Hollowed cone. (b) Trim petals as dotted line. (c) Slide calyx onto base of flower. (d) Dust, leaving a white area in the centre.

· CYNTHIA VENN ·

· LESSER PERIWINKLE ·

Field Poppy

There are many different varieties of wild poppy but the Common Field Poppy is scarlet, often with a dark centre. Still a familiar sight in fields and roadside verges June–October, but becoming rarer due to more effective seed cleaning and use of selective herbicides. The association of poppies with cornfields is ancient. Ceres, the Roman Goddess of Corn, was depicted wearing a wreath of corn poppies. In olden days, parts of the poppy were used to treat various aches and pains. A syrup made from the petals was given to babies to make them sleep.

METHOD

- Roll out bright red paste thinly. Cut four petals with a poppy cutter or template. (Ideally the two outer petals should be larger than the inner ones which will mean using two sizes of cutters or two templates).

- Thin and flute the edges and cup the centre of the petals with a ball tool. Texture the petals by pressing them against a suitable veiner. Leave each petal to set for a few minutes over a small dome or the back of a small spoon.

- Make the ovary by rolling a pea-sized ball of green paste into a cone shape. Push a hooked 24g wire through the base, flatten the top. Push many short black stamens into and at right angles to the base.

- Cut a small round disc of green paste. Mark indentations with a modelling knife like wheel spokes. Stick this disc onto the flat top with egg white. Paint fine black lines along the indentations.

- Grease the centre of a polystyrene cup from an apple tray or a special mould. Place a small red disc of paste in the centre. Moisten the disc with egg white. Lay two petals over the disc and opposite to each other with the points overlapping. Press the middle to secure firmly. Place the remaining two petals in the gaps and opposite each other, points overlapping. Press to secure.

- Push the wired centre through the petals and the disc beneath. Pull through until the centre and the stamens are sitting firmly on the petals.

- To prevent the apple cup moving away from the petals slide a paper clip onto the top of the wire immediately under the cup. Use bits of foam or something similar to support the petals until dry

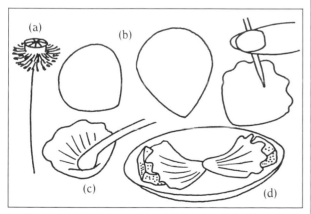

(a) Stamens inserted into centre. (b) Two sizes of petals. (c) Shaping petals. (d) Outer petals supported by foam pads and arranged in apple cup to dry.

Inner petals in position. Centre being pushed into place.

·FIELD POPPY·

Primrose

The solitary pale yellow flowers grow in clumps in woods and on grassy banks March–May. They are abundant on railway embankments where they can grow undisturbed. The generic name 'Primula' means 'First Rose' and refers to its early flowering. In the Middle Ages the Primrose was used as a cure for rheumatism and gout. The flowers were also used in the preparation of love potions.

METHOD

The Calyx

● Colour the paste a pale yellowy-green. The calyx should be made first but do not allow it to dry out before adding the petals.

● Take a ball of paste about 3mm. Roll into a cigar-shape. Hollow by inserting the cocktail stick into the pointed end of the cone.

● Make five deep cuts into the cylinder, almost to the base, with small pointed scissors. Open up and cut each one to a slender point. Press each of the sepals firmly with a cocktail stick (modelling stick) to thin them more.

● Push a hooked 26g wire through the centre. Put on one side until the petals are ready.

The Petals

● Colour flower paste a delicate yellow.

● Make a Mexican hat (see page 7). Cut out the shape with a medium Primrose cutter.

● Push pointed modelling tool (five petalled veiner if possible) into the centre, press the base of the petals against it to thin and open the throat of the flower, this also lifts the petals.

● Soften and thin the petals by laying each one over index finger and rolling a cocktail stick across each petal to thin more.

● Press petals against a veiner and mark a deep central vein on each one. Thin the back of the flower by rolling between the fingers until it is fine and dainty.

● Brush the calyx with egg white. Place the petals in the centre and close sepals around the base of the flower.

● Give a little twist here and there to the petals to give a natural movement.

● With metal tweezers, pinch a ridge along the centre of each sepal.

● Insert one stamen, this will represent the stigma, as the stamens are situated deep inside the throat and are not visible.

● Colour the centre of the flower a deeper yellow. Add a touch of pale green to the throat.

● Make small pointed buds about ¼ the size of the flower, add calyx.

● Leaves require a veiner made from a real leaf as the veining is complex.

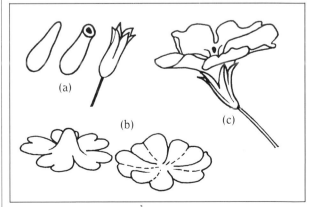

(a) Calyx. (b) Shaping petals. (c) Flower with calyx showing ridges which run the length of each sepal.

· PRIMROSE ·

Devil's-Bit Scabious

There are three types of wild Scabious, the 'Small Scabious' – which has a head made up of tiny florets with five lobes. This is the only scabious to have five petals. The 'Field Scabious' – which is the largest of the species has many florets with four lobes. The 'Devil's-Bit Scabious' is more domed, like a button. The florets are four-lobed and more of an even size but the outer florets have a larger lobe at the edge. The stamens are not really visible but each floret has a pink anther which stands higher than the head of the flower. The flower head is cupped by pointed green bracts. The Scabious flowers June–October.

METHOD

- Make a calyx with green paste. Roll into a Mexican hat and cut out shape with a daisy cutter. Insert a 24g hooked wire through the base. Make a double row of sepals by cutting a second shape with a daisy cutter and sticking it on top of the first.

Outside ring of florets

- Take a ball of mauve paste 2–3mm.

- Roll into a cone shape. Make a deep cut about half way down the length of the cone. Cut each half in two again (4 chunky petals). Cut 3 of the petals short leaving one long one.

- Press a small ball tool or a glass headed pin into the short petals to thin and shape. Thin the long petal by rolling back and forth with a cocktail stick.

- Stick a very fine cotton stamen in the centre to represent the anther. A piece of fine dried grass is excellent for this purpose.

- Brush the edge of the calyx with egg white. Stick this floret to the edge with the large petal overhanging and the pointed base towards the centre of the calyx. Make more florets the same and continue laying them on the calyx until they form a circle.

- The inner florets are smaller and the lobes are all the same size. Take a 2mm ball of paste. Roll into a small cone. Cut into four sections as before. Open out and thin with a small ball tool. Insert fine cotton or dried grass for anther.

- Brush the centre of the ring of florets with egg white. Form an inner ring with the smaller florets which should be standing upright. Continue until the central area is filled with small florets.

- Use '0' icing tube (tip) and deep pink icing to pipe the tips of the anthers.

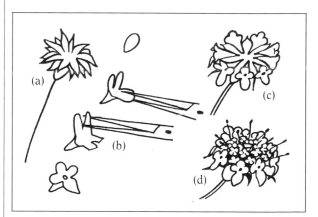

(a) Calyx. (b) Cutting petals. (c) Arranging outer petals. (d) Completed flower.

· CYNTHIA VENN ·

·SCABIOUS·

Winter Snowdrop Cake

A delicate cake for Winter or early Spring. The double row of floating extension work represents the frost and sharply contrasting colours of that time of year.

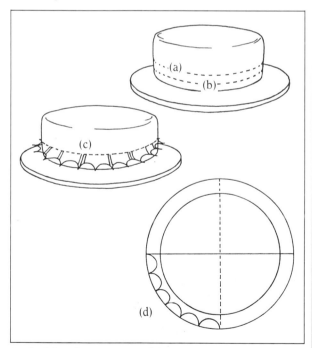

(a) Guideline for upper row of extension work. (b) Guideline for lower row of extension work. (c) Supporting threads. (d) Scalloped bridge.

Method for an 8″ (20cm) cake

● Make a template for bridgeless extension work by drawing an 8″ (20cm) circle. Draw another circle 9″ (22.5cm) in diameter, around the first circle. Divide into four. Mark off evenly-spaced sections around the outside circle and draw small scallops as illustrated. Place non-stick film over the pattern and pipe the outline of one-quarter of the scalloped sections with a No·1 tube (tip) and Royal icing.

● You will need four of these for each band of extension work but it is best to make more to allow for breakages. Allow to dry. Mark a line around the cake at the required height for the upper edge of the bottom row of extension work. Note the chosen depth of the band of extension work. Mark a second line above it for the top layer of extension work.

● Place the cake and its board on a second cakeboard, the same size. Fix the 'L' brackets in between the boards as shown in the diagram and adjust to the height required for the bridge.

● Lift the bridge carefully and place in position around the base of the cake. Use 'L' brackets to support it. Join the four sections by butting them together and securing them with a dot of Royal icing.

● Attach a narrow green ribbon just above the top guideline before starting the extension work.

● With a 00 tube (tip) pipe groups of 6−8 threads from the guideline to the bridge to act as supports while the extension

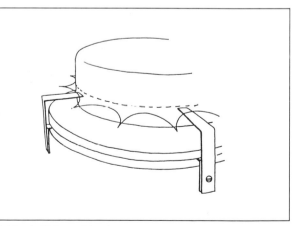

Bridge held in position by props.

work is being piped. When these are dry the brackets may be removed.

- Pipe the extension work all round, removing the piped supporting threads as you go if they are not perfectly even.

- Set the brackets for the top layer so that the band is the same depth as the lower one. Assemble the bridge as before. Pipe extension work neatly from the top guideline

down to the suspended bridge, cleaning off with a damp brush if necessary.

- Finish the edge with tiny dots of dark green.

- Make snowdrops matching the colour of the leaves with the ribbon and the piped edging.

Note: 'L' brackets by Linda Wong.

Snowdrop

The Snowdrop flowers January—March in damp woodland and meadows. It was once known as 'The Fair Maid of February'. This was connected with an old custom of celebrating the Feast of Purification of S^t. Mary on 2nd February. The village maidens would adorn themselves with snow-drops on that day as a symbol of purity.

The snowdrop has greyish-green lance-like leaves. The single drooping blossoms have three spreading white sepals which are longer than its three green tipped petals. A small leaflike spathe covers the tip of the flowering stem to protect it as it pushes up through the snow. As the flower matures the spathe which is very fine in the centre will split at the tip.

METHOD

- Moisten a piece of 28g wire with egg white and stick a tiny ball of white paste onto the hooked end. Insert short fine yellow stamens into the paste. The flower has six stamens but unless they are very fine you may need to use less.

- Roll out some white paste. Cut the petals with cutter (b). Soften the edges and cup the centre with a small ball tool. Moisten the centre of the petals with egg white and slip over the wire, moulding neatly around the stamens. Paint a green band just above, and following the line of the edges of the petals. Leave to dry.

- Most snowdrop cutters are rather narrow and the sepals sometimes look too small for the petals. To avoid this, roll the paste thicker than normal. Cut out shape (c), use the ball tool to spread the sepals and thin the edges, take care to keep the shape. Moisten the centre of the sepals with egg white and slip them over the inner petals.

- Take a ball of green paste about 3mm for the ovary. Shape into a cone and flatten the top. Brush the base of the flower with egg white. Slide ovary over the wire and stick to the base of the flower.

- Bind the wire with stem tape to thicken it. Carefully bend the wire by gripping it just below the flower head with fine tweezers so that the flower head droops.

- To make the **spathe**, roll a small sausage of green paste into a thin strip. Cut into a fine spear shape approximately $^3/_4''$ (1cm) long. Make a deep vein down the centre with a veining tool. This should be almost transparent and you may split the end if you wish. Brush the centre of the spathe with egg white. Lay the back of the flower stem against it and press, moulding the sides around the stem. The point of the spathe should be curving over towards the flower head rather like a hood.

- **The leaves** are spear-shaped with a deep central vein.

- Take a piece of green paste, press with finger and thumb to flatten it.

- Insert a piece of 26g wire into the paste, press firmly to secure. Roll the paste each side of the wire with a cable needle to thin the paste.

- Cut out long thin pointed shape with a sharp modelling knife. Thin the edges with a ball tool.

- Place leaf on a pad of foam. Press centre with a veining tool to make a deep vein, take care that the wire doesn't break through the paste. Leave to dry.

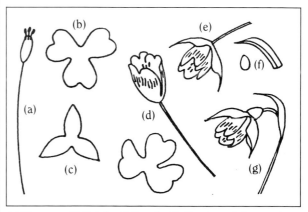

(a) Stamens. (b) Petals. (c) Sepals. (d) Petals curled around centre. (e) Sepals arranged over petals. (f) Spathe and ovary. (g) Ovary and spathe attached.

· CYNTHIA VENN ·

· SNOWDROP ·

Speedwell

There are many theories as to the origin of the name 'Speedwell' and most refer to the medicinal values attributed to the plant which range from clearing up respiratory complaints to healing wounds and curing leprosy. Another explanation refers to the fact that the flowers fall and blow away almost as soon as the plant is picked 'speedwell' was another way of saying farewell or goodbye.

The flower, which can be found in hedges, woods and grassland is bright blue with a white 'eye' in the centre. The lower of its four petals is narrower than the others. Two stamens protrude beyond the flower. The leaves grow in opposite pairs.

METHOD

● Hollow a 5mm ball of blue paste as instructions on page 6. Cut one narrow petal with small pointed scissors from the edge of the cylinder. Open out the remaining edge and cut equally into three parts. Cut off the corners to make rounded edges to the petals. Tool the edges of the petals to thin.

● Make a small hook in a piece of 28g wire. Push through the centre of the flower. Neaten the back.

● Place a tiny ball of white paste in the centre of the petals. Push firmly with the end of a cocktail stick making a small round hole, this makes the white 'eye'. Insert two white stamens, protruding beyond the flower and facing in opposite directions, right and left. Insert one short stamen in between for the stigma.

● Paint very fine dark blue veins from the centre of each petal, radiating towards the tip.

● To make the **calyx**, roll a small ball of green paste 2mm into a cone shape. Cut in two halves with small scissors, then cut each half into two again making four lobes. Pinch flat between thumb and finger then pinch into points. Slide calyx along the wire and attach to the base of the flower with egg white.

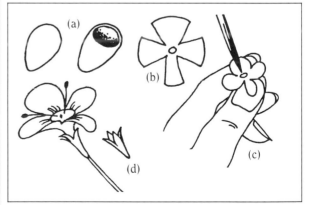

(a) Hollowed cone. (b) Cut petals. (c) Thinning petals. (d) Calyx.

· CYNTHIA VENN ·

Wood Anemone

The Wood Anemone or Windflower grows in such profusion that it carpets the woodland floor with delicate flowers of white, tinged with purple from March–May.

The petals and the sepals are not as easily distinguishable as in many other flowers and are therefore called the perianth as this refers to petals or sepals. This flower is a good example of the unpredictability of Nature since the perianth has segments numbering anything between five and nine. Six is quite a common number which I have chosen for ease of construction.

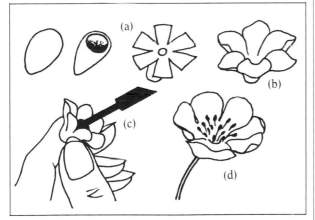

(a) Petals cut from hollowed cone. (b) Petals shaped and fluted. (c) Rounding off base with ball tool. (d) Wired flower with stamens.

METHOD

- Take a ball of white paste approximately ³/₈″ (1cm).
- Make a cone shape and hollow with a blunt cocktail stick (*see page* 6).
- Make six deep cuts. Open out and cut the tip of each section into a point.
- Soften the edges with a small ball tool. Roll cocktail stick across each petal to thin.
- Round off the base of the flower by pushing the ball tool into the centre and pressing the base gently with a finger.
- Make a hook in a piece of 28g wire. Cover it with a tiny ball of paste. Pull through the centre of the flower. Flatten out the ball of paste.
- Add a lot of fine yellow stamens set in green Royal icing. Neaten the petals if necessary and twist into a natural shape. Shade the back of the flower with pink and brush the stem pinky-brown.
- To make the **leaves**, cut out shape using template and construct as shown on pages 8–9. Use 30g wire for the leaves. Tape together three leaves, radiating out from the stem.

Viola Family: Wild Pansy

Pansies and Violets are both members of the Viola family. The main difference is in the leaves. Violet leaves are heart-shaped whereas the Pansy has longer, narrow toothed leaves. The Pansy, also known as 'Heartsease', is a symbol of remembrance. The name is derived from the French 'pensée', which means 'thought'. It was once used as a love potion. In 'A Midsummer Night's Dream', Oberon squeezed the juice of the Heartsease into Titania's eyes while she was sleeping, this made her fall in love with the first thing she saw when she woke. It has five unequal purple or yellow petals or a mixture of both with the wider one at the base and flowers April–November.

You will have greater success with the colouring of the Pansy if you start with white or cream coloured paste and add the colours by painting or dusting when the flower is dry.

- Take a ball of paste the size of a small pea. Roll into a cone shape and hollow (see page 6)
- With a pair of small pointed scissors make two snips to form the largest petal using one-third of the cylinder. Divide the remaining paste into four sections by first cutting in two halves then cutting each piece in half again.
- Trim off the square tips of these five petals, there should now be four narrow petals and one wide one.
- Roll a cocktail stick back and forth across each petal to thin and flute slightly. If the petal loses the required shape, trim it with small scissors.
- Insert a hooked 28g wire into the throat of the flower and out through the top of the pointed back, about half way along the spur, (the large petal should be at the bottom).
- The two petals at the top should stand up like ears, the two side ones angled upwards and the large bottom petal should be concave. Curve the pointed back (the spur) of the flower up towards the wire.
- Add a yellow stamen to the centre or a tiny piece of yellow paste to represent the stigma.
- **To make the calyx**, roll a tiny ball of paste into a cone shape. Hollow with a cocktail stick (thin modelling stick). Cut five points with scissors. Thin points with a small ball tool. Slip over the wire onto the base of the flower. Mould the calyx snugly, round the base of the flower.
- Pinch the base of the calyx to remove any excess paste, it must be kept fine and neat. The spur of the flower should be left free.
- When dry, bind wire with stem tape and bend stem over until flower head is hanging down. Dust with purple and yellow. Paint fine black veins radiating out from the centre of the bottom and side petals.

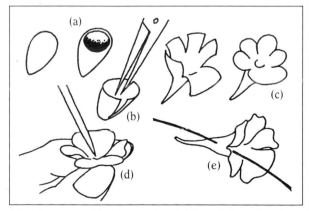

(a) Hollow cone. (b) Cutting petals. (c) Rounded petals. (d) Thinning petal over finger. (e) Wire inserted into throat; exit point halfway down spur.

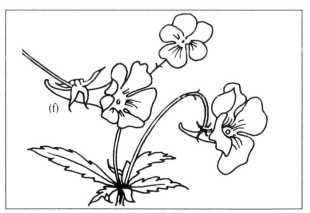

(f) Small calyx at base of stem.

·PANSY·

Sweet Violets

This cake has open-work flooded collars with matching board collars. Violets and leaves are worked into the lacy design and the surrounding area flooded. The vertical open-work corner pieces are fixed in between the collars. The board is iced with very pale mauve Royal icing to accentuate the white board collars and linework.

- The collars are designed for an 8″ (20cm) cake but could be enlarged or reduced with a photocopier for larger or smaller cakes.

- Icing for coating the cake should have glycerine added for soft cutting in proportion ¹/₂ teaspoon to 1lb mixed icing.

- Coat the cake with two or three coats of Royal icing until you get a perfect surface, allow to dry between each coat. Ice the board in pale mauve. When dry, place the template for the linework on the board and mark the lines.

- **For the collar**, use Royal icing WITHOUT glycerine. Place the collar pattern under a piece of non-stick plastic film.

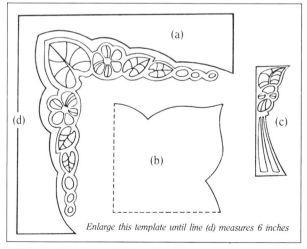

Enlarge this template until line (d) measures 6 inches

(a) Linework template (b) Top linework. (c) Corner runout.

With a '0' icing tube (tip), pipe over all outlines, finishing with the outside edge.

- Let down some of the remaining icing with water, albumen or egg white. Stir the liquid into the icing a drop at a time until the consistency is correct. If you dribble a little icing from the spatula onto the surface of the icing, the trail should disappear on the count of 10.

- Half fill a greaseproof paper icing bag with the thinned icing (no icing tube is required). Cut off the tip until the hole is the size of a No.2 tube (tip). Flood the area surrounding the lacy petals and leaves, pricking any bubbles which may form. Dry quickly near gentle heat to obtain a good surface sheen.

- You will need four collars for the top and four board collars (make spares in case of breakage). The board collars may be the same size as the top for this cake which will result in a larger gap between the board collars, leaving a convenient space for the moulded violets.

- The corner pieces are made by the same method as the collars but remember that the height should be adjusted to the height of your cake. The top of this piece should be level with the top of the cake, allowing for the thickness of the runout pieces of the board collar on which they stand. Pipe beading around the base of the cake with a No.1 tube (tip). Attach board collars to all corners by piping a line of icing on the corners of the board. Lay a collar on each corner and press gently to secure.

- Pipe board line-work with a No.2 tube (tip), overpipe this line and pipe another line by the side with a No.1. With mauve icing and a '0' tube overpipe all lines and pipe a single mauve line by the side.

- Pipe linework on top of the cake following the same method. Attach the corner runout pieces to the cake with a neat line of icing. Attach the top collars with a fine line of Royal icing (they should rest quite near to the edge of the cake and care should be taken to see that they are in line with each other).

- **To make the ornament**, make the base by flattening a 1″ (2.5cm) diameter ball of modelling paste until it is domed in the centre with thin edges. Pipe random filigree lines all over it to decorate. Arrange violets by pushing the wires into the paste, the taller flowers in the centre. Surround with leaves. When the paste has set hard, the stems can be adjusted until the flowers make a pleasing arrangement. The ornament will be free-standing and can be temporarily attached to the cake with a dot of Royal icing.

- Arrange small clusters of flowers and leaves, set in a small cushion of paste, on the board between collars.

·SWEET VIOLETS·

Sweet Violet

There are many species of wild violet, a flower which has been a symbol of love for thousands of years. The Greeks believed it to be the flower of Aphrodite, the Goddess of Love, and they made it the symbol of Athens. In the Middle Ages violets were scattered around in houses to conceal unpleasant smells. Not only do they have a lovely scent, they also produce a substance which temporarily dulls the sense of smell, thus making unpleasant odours less noticeable. The 'Sweet Violet' is very common in the British Isles. It has small fragrant blue-violet flowers from March–May and August–September. It grows in woods and hedgerows.

METHOD

This flower is constructed in the same way as the Wild Pansy.

- Take a small ball of pale violet coloured paste about 5mm. Roll into a cone shape. Hollow with a cocktail stick (thin modelling stick) and follow instructions for making the Wild Pansy.

- After pushing the hooked wire into the flower, hold the flower at the back between thumb and finger and pinch, bringing the side petals closer together and curving downwards. Curve the pointed spur up towards the wire.

- The calyx of the violet is very small and even the smallest calyx cutter would make a rather clumsy calyx. A dainty version may be made by snipping 5 points along a short length of stem tape, wrapping this around the stem at the base of the flower and arranging the points carefully.

  OR

A tiny star shape of paste could be cut out by hand with small scissors and arranged around the base of the wire. The spur should be left free.

- Dust some of the finished flowers with dark violet dusting powder, others should be left pale. Paint fine black veins on the bottom and side petals only.

- Make heart-shaped leaves using a template, or cutter, following the basic instructions for leaves on pages 8–9. Make veins with a veining tool or special veiner.

Stipules

- A pair of stipules grow either side of the stem about half way down. They are short and spear-shaped and can be cut from thin green paste and pressed on to the stem.

· CYNTHIA VENN ·

Templates

The following leaf templates are for many of the plants featured in this book. Use a photocopier set to 200% to enlarge them to correct size.

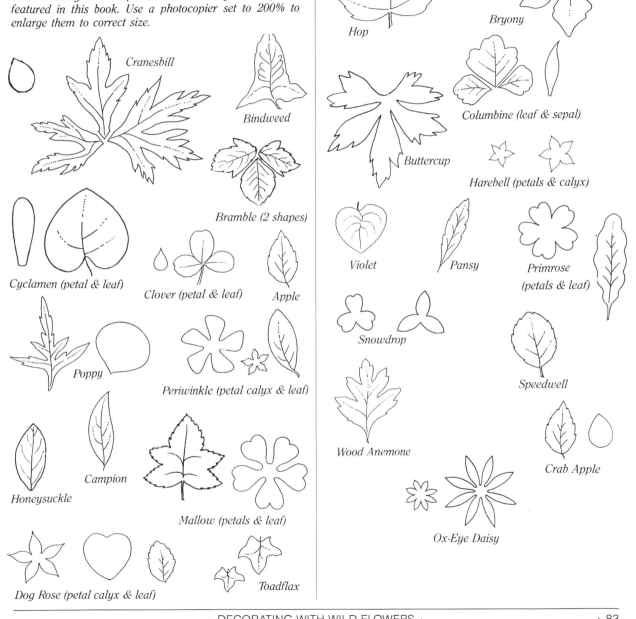

Cranesbill

Bindweed

Bramble (2 shapes)

Cyclamen (petal & leaf)

Clover (petal & leaf)

Apple

Poppy

Periwinkle (petal calyx & leaf)

Honeysuckle

Campion

Mallow (petals & leaf)

Dog Rose (petal calyx & leaf)

Toadflax

Hop

Bryony

Leaf

Buttercup

Columbine (leaf & sepal)

Harebell (petals & calyx)

Violet

Pansy

Primrose (petals & leaf)

Snowdrop

Speedwell

Wood Anemone

Crab Apple

Ox-Eye Daisy

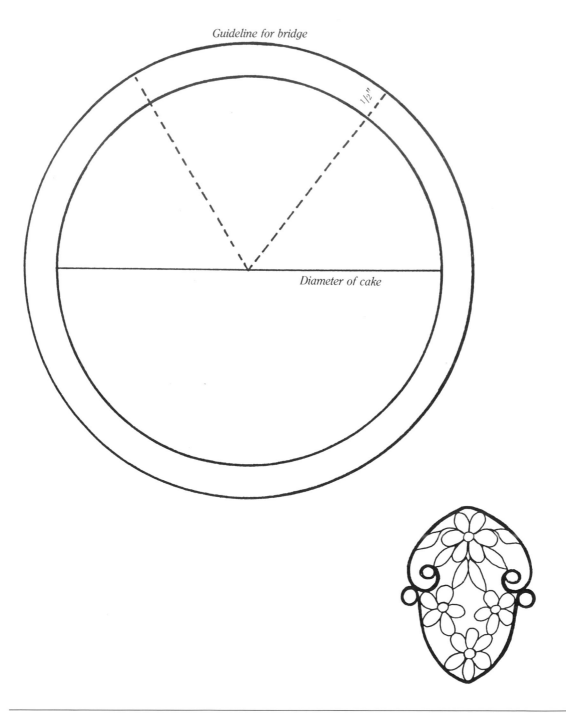

Guideline for bridge

1/2"

Diameter of cake

· CYNTHIA VENN ·